Since the advent of the
Brookhaven National Laboratory has served as the premier and most top secret research lab in the world. Shrouded in mystery since its inception, no one has been able to crack the code of secrecy surrounding it. Wade Gordon, who grew up in and around the lab and amidst its top players, now tells his personal story of how he was groomed from a very young age to share the legacy of what happened there. Beginning with Brookhaven's formative years when the Philadelphia Experiment was researched, links are revealed which tie Brookhaven directly to the the Majestic-12 documents (included in this book), the Roswell crash and the Montauk Project. Included is a description of a time chamber beneath Brookhaven Lab which was utilized to monitor the JFK assassination in order to secure funding for the continuation of the secret research.

There is vast body of data on this planet that the general public is still in the dark about. The implications of the technology developed from such research are so tremendous that they lead into any facet of creation that can be imagined. The powers of creation are wide-open. Only the limitations of our imaginations can stop us from tapping them and molding the future to our own liking. **The Brookhaven Connection** *bridges the missing gaps in our recent history and leads us on a pathway to understanding our future track. This book shifts us another ninety degrees toward the light of realization.*

C over Art:

Artist's depiction of the alien component of our consciousness holding the lightening bolt which powers the ankh of everlasting life. In the other hand is the All Seeing Eye, another area which has been relegated to the unconscious realm of man.

THE BROOKHAVEN CONNECTION

BY WADE GORDON
EDITED BY PETER MOON

SkyBooks

NEW YORK

The Brookhaven Connection
Copyright © 2002 by Wade Gordon
First printing, January 2002

Edited by Peter Moon
Cover art and illustration by Ariel Phoenix
Typography by Creative Circle Inc.
Published by: Sky Books
          Box 769
          Westbury, New York 11590
          email: skybooks@yahoo.com
          websites: www.time-travel.com/skybooks
          email for Wade Gordon:
              mindvoyager@hotmail.com

Library of Congress Cataloging-in-Publication Data

Gordon, Wade
      The Brookhaven Connection
by Wade Gordon
      256 pages
          ISBN 0-9678162-1-1
1. Time Travel 2. Aliens 3. UFO's
Library of Congress Catalog Card Number 2001 132914

This book is dedicated to my mother

ACKNOWLEDGEMENTS

To the silent heroes who came forward to help me with this book but who want to remain anonymous; and, to Don Williams, who encouraged me when times were tough; and, to Elizabeth Cooper.

CONTENTS

Other titles from Sky Books

by Preston Nichols and Peter Moon

The Montauk Project: Experiments in Time
Montauk Revisited: Adventures in Synchronicity
Pyramids of Montauk: Explorations in Consciousness
Encounter in the Pleiades: An Inside Look at UFOs
The Music of Time

by Peter Moon

The Black Sun: Montauk's Nazi-Tibetan Connection

by Stewart Swerdlow

Montauk: The Alien Connection
The Healer's Handbook: A Journey Into Hyperspace

by Alexandra Bruce

The Philadelphia Experiment Murder:
Parallel Universes and the Physics of Insanity

FORWARD

If you worked for a public relations firm, Brookhaven National Laboratory would be a nightmare to have as a client. Although they are the world's premier nuclear research facility, and their competence in physics is beyond question, Brookhaven's past negligence with regard to nuclear pollution of the local water supply on Long Island has earned them the wrath and skepticism of the citizenry. The utter disregard for the public trust would seem to be an insurmountable hurdle. Although considerable efforts are underway to try and clean up the water supply, a local survey of the population will tell you that people have much trepidation and concern about the lab because of their past track record.

Even worse than the water problem are reports of animal abuse at the laboratory. Although inhumane treatment of animals has been denied, activists have found many animal carcasses from experiments.

Brookhaven Lab is also known for its Ritalin studies which seek to "prove" that children suffering from attention deficit disorder can be "cured" by taking the new "wonder drug" Ritalin. This "scientific" finding has upset parents all across the country. It is commonly only promoted by those serving specific agendas. No one with a holistic approach recommends the use of Ritalin.

By now you might be wondering what on earth a nuclear research facility is doing experimenting on animals and dealing with complex factors of human behavior. That is a very good question, but I have not even touched the tip of the iceberg with regard to the full studies that have been conducted at Brookhaven National Laboratory over the years.

After I coauthored *The Montauk Project: Experiments in Time* with Preston Nichols, I was invited by a friend of mine to meet a lady who had a very unusual experience she thought she should share with me. This woman, who was from Switzerland, recounted her early days in the United States when she had opened up a bakery with her husband. At the time, they were struggling with English, their newly adopted language, and they had hired a young man named Billy. Although he was hired to do routine work, he ended up helping them immensely by assisting them in their understanding of the language and the customs of their new country. Quite a warm relationship developed, but in time, Billy left as this was not a career for him but only a short term job. It was well over a decade later when this lady and her husband were getting along very well with a successful business. One day, a little person walked in who looked just like Billy only he was the size of a child. The lady was happy to see what she thought must have been the son of her old friend whom she had not seen in years.

"You must be Billy's son," she said. "You look just like him."

"No," he replied. "I'm Billy! I was part of an experiment at Brookhaven Lab."

Believe it or not, this is a remarkable story that I was told. The woman who told me is very respectable. If she wanted to lie to me, she could have embellished it and made it sound even more incredible. She never saw Billy after that last mention of him.

I heard an even more remarkable story from Gail Evening Star, one of the local Montauk Indians. She met me at a Thanksgiving Day feast in honor of the Montauk tribe where I told them that their ancestors had once erected pyramids at Montauk Point and showed pictures of them. Gail was touched because no one up to that point had ever believed her when she spoke about the pyramids. She knew of them because her grandfather had told her about the ceremonies they used to perform in the compartment beneath one of the pyramids. These structures were eventually razed by the army before World War II.

As is the case with many Native American people, they often have incredible connections and experiences. Gail's mother used to write reports to J. Edgar Hoover about the secret "Bon Meetings" that were held in Yaphank, Long Island right near Brookhaven. These were Aryan activist meetings that were allowed to continue during World War II despite the crackdown on Nazi activity.

Gail's father actually worked at Brookhaven Lab during the 1960's in the capacity of a "majordomo." He met scientists and leaders from all across the world and saw to their creature comforts while they visited the lab. This man was quite popular and was constantly invited to visit dignitaries and important people abroad. Most remarkably, he told her about underground levels during the 1960's where he witnessed test tube babies being grown in laboratory conditions. Not too long after he noticed this, security tightened up. When he tried to access this area again, he was told that the experiments had been discontinued and the areas were sealed up. It is hard to believe that such experiments would be simply swept under the rug. Security became a stronger issue than it had been.

I have spoken to other people who work at the lab or who know people who work at the lab. I have been told repeatedly that nothing would surprise them where Brookhaven Lab is concerned.

If any of the above stories are even partly true, it suggests a secret cabal that is so huge that it would have to reach into the local population, the media, and local politics. One of the definitions of the word *politics* in the *Webster's New Universal Unabridged Dictionary* is "use of intrigue or strategy in obtaining any position of power or control." Only a very powerful contingent could keep such a cabal secret.

Above board behavior has never been a particular character trait that most Brookhaven politicians are known for. In fact, the Town of Brookhaven was investigated for corruption in the early 1990's by the feds. Headlines were made when a Brookhaven car dealer and real estate developer by the name of John McNamara pleaded guilty to federal racketeering charges. McNamara defrauded the General Motors Corporation out of $436 million dollars through false car loans. He admitted that he bribed town officials in Brookhaven yet no serious investigation of the politicians was ever done.

GMC is one of the biggest corporations in America. With multiple controllers and accountants to keep track of their finances, do you think that if they lost even as much as ten to fifteen million that they would not notice it? It is very hard to believe so much money could have been taken out of GMC without key executives knowing about it. There is certainly a case to be made for the possibility of GMC being involved in financing projects such as Montauk. John von Neumann, one of the key brains behind the Philadelphia Experiment and the Montauk Project, had a daughter who recently served on the Board of Directors of General Motors. Even more bizarre was a letter I received from a lady who sat in on the initial meetings of the Saturn Corporation in Tennessee. That corporation was started by GM, and there were several

14

reports of a huge underground facility with all the trappings of Montauk. The details and circumstances of this were written up in the Spring 1999 issue of *The Montauk Pulse*.

If GM was helping to fund black projects, the local District Attorney, James Catterson, was certainly not raining on anyone's parade. The feds criticized him when he convicted no one after subpoenaing McNamara, a man who freely admitted that he had bribed Brookhaven officials. It was a public outrage, but nothing was done. As a result, Thomas H. Oberle, the chairman of Citizens United for Brookhaven's Future was quoted in the paper:

"This town is not any cleaner than it was before. The ethics code is a sham."

The jury foreman, Walter A. Sewell had the following to say:

"It may be if you are an elected official and let yourself get in that position you have violated most people's conception of a code of ethics. But ethics are one thing and law is another."

When we consider the politics of the Town of Brookhaven, we have to look no further than the story of John Ford, a man who once tried to get to the bottom of some of the issues with Brookhaven Laboratory.

After retiring from his affiliation with the CIA in 1984, John Ford started LIUFON, the Long Island UFO Network, with Richard Stout, a man who worked in the Highway Department of the Town of Brookhaven. Stout was privy to many animal mutilations found along the highways in the course of his work. John enjoyed this line of investigation because he was able to call on the skills he had learned as an operative. He said it was exciting and challenging to expose the Government's cover-up.

In the Spring of 1996, John Ford met with me for the purposes of discussing a potential book wherein he would reveal the true nature of the political connections behind the Town of Brookhaven. John and his mother had been interested and active in local politics for years. He regularly collided with John Powell, a man who rose to political power through the assistance of a convicted felon by the name of Joseph Margiotta, a former Republican boss. Powell was at one time the head of the Republican party in Brookhaven Town as well as Suffolk County. The press even described Powell as the most powerful Republican in New York.

Things got so out of hand between these two that in June of 1996, Ford was arrested for allegedly conspiring to kill John Powell and two others by sneaking radium into their toothpaste. The New York media and Long Island newspapers reported the arrest with gala coverage despite the ridiculous nature of the charge. It was even stated in some news reports that experts had determined that radium in such doses is not lethal and might take several years to have an effect, if any. Ford was also charged with possession of illegal weapons, and TV news cameras panned a large collection of guns. The illegal weapons charge later had to be dropped as there was no evidence.

The information on the alleged conspiracy of John Ford came from "inside information" that has yet to be substantiated in a court of law. The search warrant itself was dated <u>after</u> the search of John Ford's premises where cans of radium were found and seized. Those who know Ford say he uses radium from time to time to calibrate his Geiger counter. Apparently, the entire arrest was a setup by a "friend" who asked Ford to move some radium cans. The "friend", who just happened to work for the Navy, was also arrested as part of the conspiracy.

Despite a goofy search warrant, John Ford was sent to jail and was *never* given a trial, let alone a speedy one.

Without a trial, no one had to take responsibility for any of their misdeeds. John Ford was declared "incompetent" and was sent to the Mid-Hudson State Psychiatric Hospital where he remains as a political prisoner to this day. Remember, his human rights were stripped away from him without him ever being allowed to stand trial. He never pled guilty either.

The entire circumstances were so unconstitutional and so completely whacky that one of America's premier newspapers, *The Washington Post*, felt it was prudent to cover the story in some respect. Consequently, the *Post* sent cub reporter Michael Colton to take on the job. He came up to Long Island and spent a few days up here interviewing Preston Nichols, myself, and whoever else had any relevant information. He was quite surprised to learn that there was such a bizarre array of supplementary information surrounding the case. This included theories of time travel as related in the Montauk Project, the crash of TWA Flight 800 being tied to particle accelerators, and a much deeper story behind John Ford than he had suspected. I gave him all the relevant issues of *The Montauk Pulse* which painstakingly explained all the legal irregularities and human rights violations concerning John Ford. Additionally, I gave him a copy of John Ford's statement to the media.

Colton did relay an interesting story upon his arrival. He phoned District Attorney, James Catterson, the man whose office put John Ford behind bars. Catterson does usually not even pick up the phone. When he heard it was the *Washington Post*, he took the call and wanted to know how the reporter felt about UFO's. When Colton told him he had an open mind, Catterson declined to be interviewed. There was no indication whatsoever that Colton was going to ask him about UFO's. There were many legal issues to discuss, but apparently, the UFO business strikes deep into the heart of county politics.

On Sunday, January 11th of 1998, the *Washington Post* ran a feature article on page F01. It was entitled "They Thought UFO's Had Landed. A Case of Hysteria, Politics, Poison and Toothpaste." The article was not complimentary of Preston Nichols, but on the whole, it could have been a lot worse. Most unfortunate was that it did not focus on the human rights issue. Definitely under the gun of his editor, Colton focused on the "kook factor." Although the UFO investigations and bizarre scenario on Long Island are factors in the overall situation, the most important point was missed. John Ford was being denied his rights. In fact, they were taken away. This issue was not even brought up or debated.

The article also indicated that John Ford had frequent phone conversations with Mona Rowe, a woman identified as a spokesperson for Brookhaven National Laboratory. Although Ms. Rowe claimed to be a sci-fi fan, she said she wished she could give Ford more interesting answers to his questions about aliens. Although she courteously invited John to visit the lab and claimed that all their doors were open to him, he declined the invitation as he feared a trap. What is particularly interesting and ironic about Mona Rowe is that the Michael Colton article identified her as accompanying the police on the night of the arrest of John Ford in June of 1996. She had suddenly transformed from a PR spokesperson to an expert radiologist to determine the radioactive content in the cannisters of radium that were allegedly in Ford's possession. Does that sound like a conflict of interest? A nuclear physicist I know looked into the records and claimed that no official report to the Nuclear Regulatory Commission was ever filed on the "illegal radium." This is illegal in itself.

Whether Rowe's role was a wild coincidence or damage control by the public relations department is not known. The idea that John Ford was given carte blanche access to all the lab is ridiculous. There are plenty of facilities in the lab which do not require tight security, but there are plenty that do. John was hesitant about going to the lab for fear of being compromised in some way.

According to an informed source, Ford was railroaded into jail and held without a trial due to the influence of the most powerful Republican in a Republican county: John Powell, the target of the alleged toothpaste plot. In reference to the obvious human rights violations, two federal officials approached Powell and indicated Ford should be allowed the protection of the law. Powell burst into a fury and said words to the effect that "this was his county." The officials politely left but realized this man was "way too big for his britches." They instigated a federal sting. As a consequence, in November 1998, John Powell was arrested, handcuffed, and jailed on charges he received payoffs for allowing illegal dumping in the Brookhaven town landfill. He was also accused of directing a massive "chop-shop" operation. The shocking news of Powell's arrest was immediately broadcast loud and clear by the New York City media and was said to rock Long Island politics to its very core. We heard no news reports of John Ford or how this might impact his situation. Nevertheless, floods of coverage by the press painted a very dark portrait of Powell, Ford's chief nemesis.

Powell was among nineteen people charged in a federal complaint stating they were part of interlocking criminal schemes that included "chop-shops," extortion, arson, obstruction of justice, and the sale of narcotics. In the court documents, he was accused of abusing his political power.

The "chop-shop" operation came as an unexpected boon to the feds. When politicians are arrested, it is not usually for something so crass as street crime. Powell had broken some new ground in this regard. Still, the illegal dumping charges loomed even larger for him because they carry heavier penalties. Powell was accused of taking at least $20,000 in kickbacks to allow illegal dumping in the Brookhaven landfill. These allegations were made by the owner of a hauling company who cooperated with the feds. The hauler said he made payments to Lapienski, the chief deputy commissioner of the Brookhaven landfill. In court documents, Powell was quoted as referring to the town dump as "my landfill."

Unlike John Ford, Powell was given a reasonable bail of $100,000 of which only ten percent had to be put up to a bail bondsman. He was released, proclaiming his innocence and vowing to win this legal battle. Fortunately for John Ford, this was a battle that Powell was not going to win. Powell suffered political disgrace and his career in this regard has been virtually destroyed. Finally, and at long last, there was some relief on the horizon. The pressure on John Ford could let up.

Several months later, Ford's attorney worked out a plea bargain with the District Attorney whereby Ford entered a plea of not-guilty by reason of mental incompetence. In accepting the plea, Judge Gary J. Weber acknowledged that it was impossible to murder someone by such means as radium in their toothpaste and directed that Ford be reevaluated mentally for the purpose of returning him to society. Ford's attorney praised the decision claiming it was "technically an acquittal." In fact, John wanted to stand trial but finally accepted the plea bargain after talking to Preston Nichols. Preston pointed out that the court had already declared him mentally incompetent, and there was nothing he could do about that. He had nothing to lose by accepting their terms. If there was any good news, it was that his pension would be restored and he might eventually be released. But, it was only after Powell's arrest and fall from power that Ford was acquitted. Any coincidence here?

On December 2nd, 1999, John Powell was found guilty of extortion by a jury for accepting $20,000 from a local trucker for access to the Brookhaven town landfill. Shock waves went through the court room as dozens of supporters gasped or cried. Outside the court, Powell was indignant and showed no signs of contrition. Questioning the fairness of the trial, he said he did learn one thing: "Innocent people go to jail." As of this writing, Powell is in a white-collar minimum security prison. The Assistant U.S. Attorney, George Stamboulidis, was humble in winning the case for the prosecution. During the trial, he said that the prosecution had "ripped the lid off. . .the corruption that was John Powell's Brookhaven."

There are other scandals in Brookhaven I could mention, but you get the point. John Ford is still incarcerated. An entire book was written about that, but publication was halted to ensure the safety of the author.

Despite the aforementioned corruption in Brookhaven, BNL was pretty much out of the loop. Certainly, they did not need the local press to cover for them because they were not personally involved in the political corruption. However, I am pointing out that the political machine in the locale was very corrupt and that it was used to curtail the investigations of John Ford.

When Long Island suffered one of the more horrible tragedies in aviation history, the sudden explosion of TWA Flight 800, the press was extremely cooperative in avoiding any confrontation of Brookhaven Lab. Although many theories have been put forward, the media refused to seriously investigate the most probable cause of the situation: a particle beam emitted from Brookhaven Lab or a related facility which activated a nuclear missile.

Hundreds of eye witnesses, many recorded on video tape, reported seeing rapid beams of light emitting from the ground and reaching the airplane as it exploded. No one, not even the press, refutes that there were many such accounts. Although the CIA attempted a disinformation campaign to discredit the witnesses, it was extremely faulty and full of holes (see *TWA - Unraveling the Cover-Up* by Jack Cashill on the internet at WorldNetDaily.com.) No rational explanations were offered about these beams of light. What is amazing is that no one even offered up a debatable proposition on this point. This is an exact point where the media can be taken to task as far as being criminally negligent. If they debated the proposition and offered up an expert to refute even the possibility of a particle beam theory, they know they would lose. Any physicist worth his salt would lose his reputation. This is why they employ the PR technique of stone cold silence. Brookhaven Lab does not have to answer to anyone because the media does not challenge them.

There were further problems with the Flight 800 investigation. The NTSB placed the time of recovery of the black boxes at 11:30 P.M. on July 24th; however, a Navy salvage report as well as a Navy message to the Coast Guard, both obtained under a Freedom of Information Act request, indicated the black boxes were found "PM 23 JUL" by the *USS Grasp*. If this was not bad enough, Congressman Michael Forbes, within two days of the plane crash, made a public announcement that the boxes were about to be brought up. He was forced to go on camera and recant, saying that he had misinterpreted what he had heard. Further investigation revealed he was at a meeting with the NTSB, FBI and Coast Guard where it was revealed that the tail section of the plane had been found and that it housed the black boxes. Although he was told the boxes would be brought up right away, there was a five to six day lag. There is no rational explanation for this.

Normally, black boxes are found through "pingers," a device which transmits an electronic signal. In the black boxes the Navy turned up, neither of the pingers were working. It is unusual for one pinger not to be working, but here both of them were not working. A seaman on the USS Grasp said the pingers were found by luck and were just lying on the sand. He also claimed the pingers did not work because they were facing down on the sand.

Not only is there a window of opportunity for the black boxes to have been shifted and replaced, the above evidence indicates that they were. Another possibility is that the pingers did not work because the electromagnetic pulse from the particle beam neutralized the pingers. Either way you look at it, there are too many unanswered questions.

One of the most disturbing incidents about Flight 800 concerned James and Elizabeth Sanders, two people who were convicted in federal court as a result of trying to find out the truth about this tragedy. Elizabeth Sanders was a flight attendant instructor for TWA at the time of the plane crash. She had acquired seat fabric from Flight 800 from a TWA pilot who was a party to the official investigation. James Sanders had the fabric analyzed and claimed that reddish-orange residue on the fabric was consistent with a residue that would be left by rocket or missile fuel. James Sanders even penned a book entitled *The Downing of TWA Flight 800*.

James Sanders' discoveries created all sorts of problems for the FBI. On August 23, 1996, the FBI announced that traces of chemicals used in explosives were found in the passenger section of the wreckage of Flight 800. Acting as if they had done a thorough investigation, they announced a few weeks later that the chemicals were the residue of a dog-sniffing bomb test conducted on June 10th by an officer of the St. Louis Airport Police. This sounded fine except for one important fact. The 747 which supposedly had been tested was scheduled to leave the airport twenty minutes after the test. This means no time to board luggage, passengers, food, and the crew. It turned out there was another 747 in St. Louis that day, but that plane was headed for Honolulu. A source inside TWA also indicated that the Airport Police had suggested two dates for when the bomb-sniffing test was done. When TWA said the plane was not there on those dates, they came up with the June 10th date. In other words, law enforcement was looking for a date that could explain the explosives rather than taking an unbiased scientific approach. When Sanders pointed out that the residue of explosives were found about the rest of the plane, the FBI claimed that explosive chemicals were leaked throughout the plane as a result of insecure containers and the like.

Sanders even wrote a second book about Flight 800 that was entitled *Altered Evidence*. He revealed how James Kallstrom, the FBI agent in charge of the investigation, said the reddish-orange residue found on the seats was nothing more than adhesive made by the 3M company. In 1998, Sanders visited the hangar in Calverton where the wreckage of Flight 800 remained. He was there to photograph evidence for his defense. To his surprise and disappointment, he noticed that the FBI had removed the seats in the section where the reddish-orange residue had been discovered. This is called altering evidence and is a criminal offense. Sanders was even able to produce an affidavit by the chemist who did tests for the NTSB. C.W. Bassett, a NASA chemist, would not state that the reddish-orange residue was in any way consistent with 3M adhesive. Under penalty of perjury, he stated that the tests he performed "did not address the origin of any reddish-orange residue. The tests I performed for the NTSB cannot answer such a question." He even said that the tests "did not identify specific elements, by quantity, within the reddish-orange residue of the sample submitted to them by Mr. Sanders."

The FBI's solution to the problems presented by James and Elizabeth Sanders was to convict them in federal court on the technicality of "taking part in theft of evidence from a crash site." It was the TWA pilot who had stolen the fabric for the Sanders. While he was the actual "thief," the FBI granted him immunity to testify against the Sanders. Otherwise, he would have been prosecuted. A witness who attended the trial said the evidence was overwhelming against the FBI and was very supportive of the Sanders. The only problem was, according to the witness, the jury was completely intimidated by the Government and were afraid to move in any other direction than conviction. The Sanders were not put in prison but were given probation. They are appealing the verdict.

Mr. Sanders is a professional journalist and by reputation a very good one. He and his wife's interest in the Flight 800 tragedy were as advocates for the public interest. Innocent people were killed and plenty of lies and inaccuracies exist in the evidence trail. In fact, they were prosecuted for seeking answers when the FBI was stonewalling the truth. Of course, this is the same FBI who supervised the Waco massacre.

Although this information does not point the finger at Brookhaven Lab specifically, it reveals that Long Island was a hot and heavy playground for vested interests who seem to stop at nothing to get their way.

Of course, there are always some people who do not believe that the media could possibly bypass such outrageous truths. Well, there is a very good reason that networks and even your "rabble-rouser" reporters like Geraldo Rivera do not honestly take on such topics (including the Montauk Project). It is because of a group called Accuracy in Media. They are a group of people who review the content of media and have an immense influence on what goes out to the press or is put on the airwaves. The people chosen for Accuracy in Media are selected by the biggest corporations in America. This group has been exposed on Free Speech TV under a documentary entitled *The Myth of the Liberal Media.*

There are further fiascoes concerning the media's coverage of airplane crashes and particle accelerators on Long Island, one of which was JFK, Jr.'s mishap. According to an eyewitness, the wiring in the plane was melted in such a manner that could only have come from a particle beam or electromagnetic pulse. When the plane was dredged up for the media to observe it, it turned out to be the wrong plane!

You can now see that a public relations firm would more than have its hands full if it had to answer to all the strange goings on at BNL or on Long Island. Fortunately for BNL, they have the cooperation of the local media and politicos. Nonetheless, the public has given them a hard time when given the opportunity. During summer tours at Brookhaven Lab, brochures and tour guides inform the public not to ask about aliens or if they have aliens at Brookhaven. They indicated they receive many such questions and do not have anything of the kind there. From a positioning point of view, denying allegations puts one in a very defensive posture. The best tactic to take with public relations is to aggressively promote the good you are doing in the environment. With regard to this point, Brookhaven National Laboratory does get very good coverage and high regard in the press for their pure nuclear research. On the controversial issues, they have a tendency to remain stone cold silent. Although the media has taken them to task on the radioactive pollution of the Long Island water system, other topics are left to drift in the wind.

What is really behind the high drama on Long Island and the enormous resources that have been expended to cover up the truth? Brookhaven Lab sits as the mystery of mysteries on Long Island, the island of mysteries.

Long Island is not only home to the pinnacle of nuclear research but it is at the forefront of genetic engineering, microwave technology, and a host of other technologies most people have never heard of. How did it all happen?

This book, *The Brookhaven Connection*, is the testimony of one person who grew up in and around Brookhaven Lab and routinely talked to scientists who were clandestinely listed as maintenance workers in order to obscure their true operations. It is a real life story designed to give us a glimpse of how secretive forces worked behind the scenes to build a massively complex technology center that has no limits. Hopefully, it will fill in some holes for those of us who have tried to understand that mystery of mysteries which is Brookhaven.

INTRODUCTION

Brookhaven National Laboratory (BNL) is located in the quiet suburban community of Upton, New York. To the general public, BNL is the preeminent multidisciplinary research laboratory of the United States. It is the site for high profile television documentaries on neutrons and neutrinos, charged-particle and photonuclear reactions, and the latest developments in particle physics. In addition, Brookhaven National Laboratory Public Affairs office provides grade-school children and the general public guided tours of the laboratory. All this exposure would lead one to believe that at Brookhaven there is nothing to hide. However, beneath the photogenic labs and the carefully orchestrated images of white smocked clinical researchers with identification badges carefully following security procedures, there is a maze of subbasements where the real research takes place: exploring hyperspace and time travel.

This is the story of how an 8 year-old-boy discovered what was really going on at Brookhaven. It is my own highly personal account of finding the bits and pieces of a puzzle that have come to be known as "Project Rainbow" and reveals the drama of a military-industrial-collaboration so astounding that I was told by adults that dire consequences would ensue if I should ever reveal what I saw and heard. This became the greatest source of my emotional distress for the last 32 years until now. But now, as an adult, I have found the courage and the evidence I did not possess as a frightened child when I was intrigued by the description of green fog and a disappearing naval ship. This is an eyewitness account of facts frozen in time and memory for 32 years that are now coming to light.

1

CENTRAL ISLIP

My story begins in 1968 when I lived with my mother and two sisters in Central Islip on Long Island, New York. One Saturday morning, my mother took the three of us to the house of a friend in Ronkonkoma, New York. This friend, an assistant researcher, worked at Brookhaven National Laboratory which was a reasonably short drive away. Every Tuesday, Thursday, and Saturday, the adults would socialize together at each others' houses. It was a close-knit and tight-lipped community in the central portion of Long Island. While the men played cards in the basement or kitchen, the women had their coffee klatches in the living rooms and dining areas. The children were dismissed to play on the sun porches, decks, or backyards. The kids were given strict orders not to disturb the men. To a youngster my age, anything off limits was a thing that had to be investigated.

On this particular day, my mother sent me to a neighbor's house where I would play with Brian. She said she would call me later. After about an hour and a half at Brian's house, I became bored. I wandered back to where the mysterious card games were being held and sneaked into the front door. The women were busy talking in the

31

kitchen. Slipping past them, I moved through the living room and into the hallway. To the left and under the staircase that led upstairs was the basement door. Opening the door to a dark staircase, I heard voices and saw a lighted area off to the right of the bottom of the steps. As I started down the wooden stairs, I could see a bulb over a card table far off to the right. Although this was an awkward vantage point, I could observe and hear everything. I sat and listened to a conversation that was low and muffled. Words like "draw," "raise," and "call," with the occasional expletive, echoed off the basement cement walls.

Besides the poker jargon, they used other words, too, but these were seemingly out of place. Although the words and phrases they used were quite meaningless to me at the time, they have remained embedded in my memory, fused together by the excitement of that moment where I sat and listened to adult conversations which I was not supposed to be privy to. One voice used the term "Oscillator Synchronization." Another said "Phase Angle Variance." A third voice came through the static of card shuffling and the tinkle of shot glasses and said "green fog." Interspersed between these terms, which I vowed to look up later, came phrases and fragments of sentences.

"Did FDR really know about this Zero Time Reference Generator?

"Einstein was shrewd in saying that the Unified Field Theory didn't work."

"Such technology in the wrong hands could mean an end to our way of life."

"It was Tesla's idea, not von Neumann's."

"There would be hell to pay if people ever found out that 'Uncle Sam' had this kind of technology in use during World War II."

In my reconstruction of these fragmented pieces of conversation, I have been able to determine the time period the men were discussing. There was the incident in the Philadelphia Navy Yard and certain unexplainable meteorological phenomenon such as "green fog." Finally, there were the horrific references to men who appeared to be stuck in walls, bulkheads, and staircases that took place in 1943. Not until recently did I become aware that this information contained such important revelations. Although my researches have led me to unbelievable speculations and conclusions, the quality of my recollections are absolutely clear.

2

THE UNIFIED FIELD

After the startling revelations at the card game, I wanted to learn more about the ship that disappeared into the green fog. At the time, I was in the third grade attending Margaret L. Mulvey Elementary School (formally the Boulevard Avenue School) in Central Islip, New York. I waited until Library Day and set about the task of finding out more about the words "Unified Field Theory" and "Einstein." Before I begin, I should confess that I had taken a reading placement test the previous year and the proctor had to double check the results. The test administrators could not believe the score. I was reading on the ninth grade level, and I was only in the third grade. I do not consider myself any smarter than the next guy. To me, I just liked to read and the test was easy.

As the library at my school did not have any books on Einstein or the Unified Field theory, I went to the Central Islip Public Library. From there, I was told to go to the East Islip Public Library located on Main Street in East Islip. Walking up to the librarian, I asked her about books on Einstein, and she directed me to the card catalog. I started sifting through the cards to find anything I could about Einstein's Unified Field Theory.

In the book *What Einstein's Theory of Relativity Means To Me*, I was surprised when I read a reference to the Unified Field Theory as not being proven. How could that be? The men who played cards that night had talked about it as if it were real. Then, I remembered more of what they said. I remembered a name that began with a "T" and ended with "a". It had two syllables. I also remembered something about "coils." I knew I needed to learn more about the Unified Field Theory because I believed that there was a connection. The only way I could do this was to sneak into another card game to listen and learn. This time I would take notes.

3

UNCLE GEORGE

The next card game was on a Tuesday evening. It began at 7:00 p.m. and ended about 10:30 p.m. or 11:00 p.m. This time, we went to Hauppauge and the home of my Uncle George who worked at Grumman in Bethpage, New York. I found out later that he had designed the Lunar Module's (LM) landing struts.

My uncle was a fascinating character. In his basement was a workshop where he had working models and some of the early prototypes and mock-ups of the LM. When I was alone with him, he revealed a few details about his project, but it was TOP-SECRET. Whenever there were other people around, he would not talk about it and made me promise not to repeat anything he said. He often hinted that there was more he wanted to tell me but would never elaborate on this until later in his life. At that point, as if he were giving a confession, he revealed to me that someone needed to know that a faction of the U.S. Government and the military-industrial-complex were collaborating on projects that suggested we were not alone in the universe. He said that he confided in me because although I was precocious enough to remember certain details, I was young enough not to be believed should I tell some of my friends. He thought of me as a time-release capsule, hoping that I would remember these things later in life and take up the search for the truth. He ended his disclosure with an admonition to steer clear of MAJES-TIC-12 and said they have the power to make anyone or anything disappear.

My plan was a simple one. Get away from the other kids, grab a paper and pen, and sneak into the card game. This card game, like the other one, was played in the basement. What was different this time was that, instead of all day Saturday, it was in the evening. This meant that it would be a shorter game and I would have less time.

As the evening began, I played a board game with the other kids in an upstairs bedroom and lost on purpose so I could get away. Soon afterwards, I made my way down to the basement. As before, the room was dark except for the light above the card table. The men were absorbed in their card game. Out of the five men present, the only one that I recognized was my Uncle George. The other four were new to me. As these men spoke, they indicated they were agitated about something. I surmised that it was about an experiment. Evidently, an experiment had gone haywire just the day before. This time, the men were using different terms and phrases.

One scientist named Ed said, "But we didn't have the right. Its unethical."

The others argued with him about "duty," "patriotism," and "National Security." I also heard other terms like "magnetic synchronization" and "Tesla coils" as well as comments about weather anomalies caused by an agitation of sea water by powerful ultra sonic waves which produced "sonoluminessence" or "green mist."

At the time, my spelling was good, but my phonetics were a little weak. My notes, which I later transferred to a composition book and have saved, record that my note taking abilities for a 3rd grader were fairly reliable, but what they contained was too unbelievable, even for me now. I will reveal that there was a reference to "restrictions on moon-base activities" due to "preexisting agreements with another 'race' more advanced which had already established their own 'terra-forming outposts' on Earth's moon and on Mars."

I was an avid science fiction and comic book reader and had a precocity toward science projects which were mostly in biology. Nonetheless, these revelations were to me like the unearthing and translation of the "Rosetta Stone" or the "Dead Sea Scrolls." I was enraptured by the mysteries these words unfolded as well as by the emotional distress under which these engineers and scientists were working. They were undoubtedly worried and felt overwhelmed by the implications of the secrets they were under oath to protect and never disclose. My uncle must have felt the same way. In this manner, I became his "tape recorder" and, in a similar way, the recorder of these men's distress.

Personally, I did not know what to think about these revelations. My mind at that age could not fathom the implications of such knowledge. I simply took my note pad and its hastily scribbled notes and made my way back to join the rest of the kids upstairs.

4

COLUMBIA UNIVERSITY

Here I was, a young kid with a composition book full of huge terms that I could not even begin to decipher. Not only was I uneducated in physics, I did not even know what physics was. If I asked questions about physics to any of my mother's friends, they would know that I had been eavesdropping on their private conversations. I had to be very careful.

Out of the blue, a solution came to me. Every weekday morning, at 6:30 a.m., I watched a television program entitled *Sunrise Semester* on WCBS channel 2. I loved this program and wished that I had studied this stuff in grade school. One day, when watching a particularly thought-provoking program on humanities and philosophy, I noticed that the credits stated that the program was produced by Columbia University in New York City. Although I knew nothing about Columbia University save for its location, a plan began to surface.

I soon went to the public library and looked up the university's address and an official of the Physics Department. Next, I wrote him a letter telling him a little bit about myself and my interest in science. I ended the letter with a question: "What was Einstein's Unified Field Theory?"

41

The reply I received was something that I was not even remotely prepared for. The Physics Department official, Dr. John Stevens, sent back a ten page explanation of Einstein's researches and a summary of the application of his field theory and stated that Einstein was working on it but did not complete it before his death in 1955. I was expecting to be ignored or blown off, but this was an eye opener. He did not say that I was too young. In fact, he encouraged my research and invited me to visit him at his office. When I showed my mother the letter, she contacted him and set up an appointment for me to meet him. Right then and there, I made the conscious decision not to pursue the card games until I could figure this thing out.

It was not until recently that I received permission from Dr. Stevens to discuss his part in my personal ordeal, but he still did not want his real name used. He has since retired and now feels that me talking about this would no longer endanger his life as it could have back in the sixties.

5

DOCTOR STEVENS

In order for me to meet Dr. Stevens, my mother took the day off from work and had me stay home from school so she could take me into New York City (back then, we called it "the city"). The city was about sixty five miles away, and we took the Long Island Rail Road (LIRR) into Pennsylvania Station (Penn Station). I had been on the train plenty of times before so this was not new to me. We arrived at Penn Station located beneath Madison Square Garden and took a cab to Columbia University. On the way over, I remember having talked my mother into taking me to the American Museum of Natural History on the way back.

After finding Dr. Stevens' office, we waited until he was ready to receive us. Dr. Stevens looked like the typical academic, complete with a corduroy jacket and elbow patches. The first thing he said to me was, "I wish that my students were as interested in science as you are." He then asked me where I found out about Einstein and his Unified Field Theory. I lied and said I had heard about him on TV. Although I did not think he believed me, he did not let on. After giving me a protractor and a stack of books, he told me to read them cover to cover. I had never seen a protractor before and asked him what it was. He said it was a device used in advanced mathematics and mentioned that he had included a book by Dr. Isaac Asimov on its instruction. I had no idea what he was talking about. Dr. Stevens also told me to read Isaac Asimov's *Words of Science* then proceed to Dr. Asimov's *Understanding Physics Volume 1*.

Dr. Stevens said, "Dr. Asimov will give you a good foundation to build upon. He writes books for the layman."

Even though I had no idea what the protractor was for, I thanked him for it and the books. He next asked me if I had anything else to ask him about.

"I have a few questions to ask you," I replied. "Who are Tesla and von Neumann? And, what is Phase Variance and Oscillator Synchronization?"

He jotted this down and said he would get back to me. I thanked him again for the books and for giving me his time. After he shook my hand, my mother and I left his office. On the way back to Penn Station, we stopped at the American Museum of Natural History and then ate at an automat. We caught the train and went home. I couldn't wait to get home and read these books.

6

TOP SECRET

I now had tools with which to explore my questions. After devouring the books cover-to-cover, I soon came to a startling conclusion: either the material I learned at the card games was far superior than my books could discuss, or the material was top secret. Only much later did I come to realize that it was both.

A turn of events began when my mother received a phone call from Dr. Stevens. She told me that Dr. Stevens was insistent on seeing me again. He further stated that if it was not possible for us to come in to the city, he would come to our house. Accordingly, my mother made arrangements for him to come for dinner.

When Dr. Stevens arrived, he was visibly shaken. He kept chain smoking cigarettes. In fact, he would light one before the last one was even finished. In almost no time, he asked my mother for her permission to speak to me privately. After she gave her okay, Dr. Stevens and I went downstairs to my bedroom to talk. On the way down, Dr. Stevens kept repeating that his department receives government funding and that he had his career and tenure to think about. I did not really understand exactly what he was driving at, but I saw that it was very important to him.

Next, he sat down and said, "You know those questions you asked me about? Von Neumann and Tesla? I checked with a colleague [Author's note: to whom I shall refer to as Dan Peterson] of mine at Princeton. He works at the Institute for Advanced Study. This is where Einstein finished his career."

In no uncertain terms, Dr. Stevens told me not to ask about von Neumann, Tesla, Phase Angle Variance, and Oscillator Synchronization. Further, he told me not to speak of these things over an unsecured phone line, that our conversation never took place and added that if I knew what was good for me, I would just forget all about it. Dr. Stevens then said that this information was above TOP SECRET and that he did not have the clearance to talk about it.

"Does this have anything to do with MAJESTIC-12?" I asked.

At the mere mention of that name, Dr. Stevens' eyes bulged and his face turned white.

"What does this mean?" I asked him.

"Where on earth did you hear about them?" he replied. "And don't tell me you heard about them on TV ... on second thought, don't tell me, I don't want to know."

After he calmed down and the shock wore off, he went on to say that he would like to talk to me about these things, but we would have to find a way to communicate without letting anyone realize that we were talking. He concluded by saying that he was not put off by the warning, but he was shocked to learn that a boy in the third grade knew about a portion of the U.S. Government that even the Congress and the president either did not know about or publicly acknowledge. He next said that my mother would probably start to worry about where we were and that we should head on to dinner.

"Let me think about how we should best proceed next," he assured me.

We both went upstairs and ate dinner with the rest of my family and acted as if nothing had happened.

From this day on, Dr. Stevens and I continued to correspond, and I have counted on his friendship and counsel for many years. He played a big part in the events that continued to unfold in my life.

7

A NEW PLAN

A decision had to be made whether to heed the warning from Dan Peterson or to keep prodding onward in search of the truth. With thirty-two years of hindsight, I probably would do the opposite of what I actually did. At the time, I was a scrappy kid with a permanent set of bruised knuckles. I went forward into the unknown and enjoyed every second of it. The only problem I had was that I could not tell anybody exactly what I was doing. My only confidant was Dr. Stevens, and I was not completely sure that he was on my side.

In the back of my mind was the haunting vision of a destroyer escort surrounded by green fog and disappearing into space. To me, this was an exciting premise and sure beat the hell out of comic books and TV. The citizens of the U.S. were in turmoil over the conflict in Vietnam and the generation gap was becoming more and more evident. For a time, my life went back to normal for a kid in the third grade.

Eventually, there was another adult "get together" coming up on a Saturday, and I needed a plan of action. About this time, my mother had bought me a portable G.E. reel-to-reel tape recorder. It ran on four D-cells and had

3-inch reels which meant that the recording time would be about five minutes. It actually took a year and a half before I purchased a cassette recorder so that I could then record the whole card game. With my first tape recorder, my plan was to record my impressions and utilize it in conjunction with my notes. I was now ready to make the most of what I had to work with.

8

SECURITY LEAK

It was Saturday and time for another "get together." This time, we were going to a home in East Islip or so I thought. When we got there, it was announced that it was a beautiful day and we would be going to Heckscher State Park. The moms and the kids were packed in three cars and sent ahead for a cookout at the park. I later found out that the men wanted to have some "private time" to discuss their work without the kids around.

Many years later, through discussions with Dr. Stevens, I discovered why there was a sudden change of plans for a picnic. Dr. Stevens phone inquiry to Dan Peterson at the Institute for Advanced Study had triggered off a security alert. Either Dan Peterson had reported the phone call from Dr. Stevens to his superiors or the Institute for Advanced Study was under phone surveillance. It must have been the latter because Dr. Stevens continued to receive information from Dan Peterson but in a round-about sort of way. A mail drop was established using a post office box. Direct communication via phone lines was not possible because of the monitoring.

There were many reasons for the very tight security. After all, this was 1968 and teenagers were starting to "turn on and drop out." The Government rationalized that, because of the Cold War, they did not want to tip off their enemies about what they were up to. This was before the internet when the primary source of communication was the telephone and radio. These types of communication were easy to compromise. It was the era of "spy versus spy" and blue smoke and mirrors.

The picnic at Heckscher Park turned out to be a lot of fun. I got to play with the other kids and the moms had their coffee klatch. As for my own surveillance project with the men, I had to wait until the following Tuesday for another opportunity to conduct my research.

The "spy games" I conducted during my youth were a lot of fun, but I cannot say that I understood the immense significance of what I was hearing. I was too intent on probing into the mysteries of adulthood. The private conversations I heard, delivered in hushed tones, would keep any kid spellbound. The stress and anxieties that came through their vocalizations electrified me even though I did not clearly hear or understand all of the words. It was a time during which I became obsessed by their stories, even riveted by them, and obsessed by what I saw as the absolute necessity to record and observe even more. You could say that surveillance became a hobby of mine.

The men at these games were between the ages of 30 and 55. They had lived through an historic period in the history of America and the world which featured the advent of the airplane and the rocket as well as the earliest computer. They had witnessed the second half of an explosion of inventions and inventive genius that began with electricity, light bulbs, and the telephone and pro-ceeded to vacuum tubes used in radio and television as well as radar technology. Parallel to this was Einstein's theory of the photo electric effect, $E=MC^2$ and, finally, the

Atom Bomb. They had also lived through the dramatic period of World War II.

I could not help but notice that one of the men at the card game was senior in rank or position to the other members of the group. The other men seemed to listen to him almost as raptly as I did. He seemed to be something of an historian as regards strange or top secret projects. The other men questioned him about events that had occurred many years before. By their questions, I could tell that they must have thought it possible to cause an object to "disappear" in one place and "reappear" in another. This could be done either by creating an illusion that would cloak or disguise the object or by actually causing the object to be transformed to another level or dimension through the use of "Magnetic Resonance."

The man in the know I will refer to as "Mr. J." During his life, he asked the men sitting around the table to honor his request of anonymity. At this particular time, I deem it best not to reveal his true identity for reasons that have to do with the surviving members of his family.

9

MR. J

It was Tuesday as we headed back to East Islip for another "get together." As my mother was driving, she said Mr. J was a very important man and mentioned that he had a lot on his mind after attending a big meeting in Washington, D.C. I was instructed to stay out of his way and not bother him with a lot of questions. Either my recollections were not straight in my mind or I did not hear her properly when she said that he was from Commack or Amityville. After further investigation, I found out that he was from Commack.

When we arrived in East Islip, the men were playing cards in the kitchen. This was a minor setback for me as I preferred that the card game was held in the basement. That way, I had more room to maneuver and it made it easier for me to sneak in unseen. With the thought of the mysterious Mr. J stirring in my brain, I stole a peek into the kitchen. I recognized three of the men playing cards, but the one that caught my eye was the one I assumed to be the mysterious Mr. J. By the way he commanded the attention of the group, I could tell he was their leader. It was not that his appearance was striking, but it was his presence at the table, as if he was holding court. Mr. J was in control of the game and also the center of the group's conversation. It was as if every player held onto his every word and gesture. He was a big man; not tall, but a husky he-man type. Mr. J was usually very quiet and never shared his feelings. It was obvious to me that the rest of the group looked up to him; not because he was older but for his inner strength. He had thinning salt-and-pepper hair and wore a white long sleeve shirt with the sleeves rolled up to his elbows. This look was complemented a pair of black suspenders.

As Mr. J smoked a big stogie, I could hear his slow-measured-speech command the group. I had a choice to make. Either I could go outside and look through the window, but not be able to hear anything, or put on a brave face and go into the kitchen and pray that I would not be noticed. I chose the latter because of my past experience at the card games. I thought that they might not notice my presence. Even though Mr. J was obviously in control of the game, he saw me immediately but did not say anything. He simply turned his head and nodded to me. The men continued talking and playing as if nothing had happened. They were talking about a payroll problem.

In response to this, Mr. J said, "I'll handle it and consider it done."

After a few minutes, I started feeling uncomfortable sitting there and decided to leave. As I got up, Mr. J stopped what he was saying to the men, looked in my direction, and signaled me over to him.

"Kid, I have to admit that you've got balls and I admire it," he chuckled.

Then Mr. J stopped and looked me in the eye as he said, "Listen, kid. No more secret-agent games and sneaking around. If you want to sit in, it's okay by me. Just come on in anytime and make yourself at home. There's no secrets among friends. Just one thing though. Anything we say here stays here. You got that kid?"

I timidly nodded my head as Mr. J reached out his bear of a hand. I slowly moved my hand forward and shook his.

Mr. J turned to face the group, cleared his throat, and said, "Gents, this kid is welcome to any of our meetings. Treat him with respect like he's one of our own."

I have to admit that I was stunned at the revelation that I was found out. I thought I had been more careful than that. I did not learn until much later that Mr. J wanted me there. He was looking for a person with an interest in the subject matter but, more importantly, a person he could trust with important information. Mr. J wanted their story told to the public some day but not until the people involved were either retired or dead.

Mr. J had figured out that I was the security leak who had talked to Dr. Stevens. In fact, this was the event that "sold" him on me. He surmised that if I had the brains to contact Dr. Stevens, I was good enough to join his team. To this day, I do not know exactly how they connected me to Dr. Stevens. As I know that he did not talk to anyone, I assumed that my mother told Mr. J.

An admonition I can give to prospective investigators is exactly what Mr. J told me: If you want to pursue this type of inquiry, remember that there are professionals with many years of experience looking at you with a vast arsenal of tools at their disposal. These professionals will know more about you than you realize while you will not even have a clue that you are being targeted.

For the time being, and for many years to come, I was safe from the watchful eye of "Big Brother." Mr. J's associates watched out for me and made sure that nobody suspected my relationship to them. I am very thankful that they did this for me. Once I was welcomed into their inner circle, my life began to change. I was soon given the answers to my questions. But, after these questions had been answered, the door was flung open for more to come crashing in.

10

PROJECT RAINBOW

When another "get together" day came around, my mother acted very differently towards me. I asked her about what was going on, and she just smiled and said, "You will find out later."

She only hinted that I had made quite an impression on Mr. J and that he had specifically asked that she bring me that day. When we arrived at the house in East Islip, my mother walked me into the card game (held in the kitchen). I felt like I was the guest of honor at a party. The game stopped and Mr. J welcomed me. He then signaled me to sit on a chair next to his stating that I could not play cards but could listen to what the group had to say. He even indicated that I could take notes and ask questions.

Mr. J had whispered in my ear that he had paid Dr. Stevens a visit. He then turned to face the group and said, "I'd like to have been the fly on the wall when that 'long-haired intellectual' found out what is really going on. That guy is smart enough to realize which way the wind blows and knows enough to keep his big trap shut."

Mr. J ended his comments on the matter by saying, "That Stevens guy likes to have steady money coming in so he won't upset the apple cart."

After reviewing my notes, I had no idea what these statements meant, but I gathered that it was okay to write to Dr. Stevens.

Mr. J went on to say, "People will really find this hard to believe, but a ship did indeed disappear. Or to be exact, it became transparent. And Einstein was there and was the person who made it all possible with his Unified Field Theory. The Government covered up all the tracks that led back to him because he was so high profile. It was a lot easier to do back in those days with World War II going on."

Mr. J continued, "It was all Einstein's idea because he was the 'thinker' and it was up to Tesla, 'the builder,' to realize Einstein's vision. It all began around 1918 when Einstein completed his Unified Field Theory. He did not realize its ramifications but Tesla did. He constructed a radio to communicate to our 'friends.' Einstein tried to put the 'genie' back into the bottle by announcing that his theory wasn't complete. To an extent, he succeeded. The general public assumed that it wasn't complete, but the people in the know like FDR knew better."

Tesla was described by Mr. J as a brilliant tinkerer and that people thought he was crazy, but this was just an act to ensure his privacy. Back then, I did not have a clue who Tesla was, but I assumed he was important. I also did not know who FDR was, but after further research, I determined that FDR meant Franklin Delano Roosevelt, the 32nd President the United States, from 1933-1945, who was also a good friend of Nikola Tesla.

"Project Rainbow," according to Mr. J, was created to test Einstein's Unified Field Theory. It was all very hush-hush. The idea was to make a ship invisible to the enemy in response to the vast sinking of Allied ships by Nazi U-boats. The project had a cover story. It was that the experiment was being conducted to test a method of degaussing. According to the Navy's official position, degaussing is a process in which a system of electrical cables are installed around the circumference of a ship's hull, running from bow to stern on both sides. A measured electrical current is passed through these cables to cancel out the ship's magnetic field. Degaussing equipment was installed in the hull of Navy ships and could be turned on whenever the ship was in waters that might contain mines. This was the defensive rationalization the Navy used when asked what the equipment aboard the *USS Eldridge* was for. It was a plausible answer and succeeded in confusing reporters, researchers, or other naval personnel who attempted to find answers.

The first experimental run by Tesla was a success, but it did not really yield the effect the Navy wanted. That brought von Neumann on board to run the project. This was better for the project because Tesla was having problems with his health and von Neumann was an excellent "problem solver." It was von Neumann who pushed the program forward. Mr. J concluded by saying that the second experiment under von Neumann's direction was a success, but it had unexpected side effects. The ship became transparent, and when it reappeared, sailors had materialized inside the bulkheads of the ship. The Government stamped it as a failure and secretly moved the project to Brookhaven National Laboratory after the conclusion of World War II.

After several conversations with the rest of the gentlemen present at the card game, I discovered that Mr. J had succeeded Dr. John von Neumann at BNL (Brookhaven National Laboratory). But on that night, it was getting late. I had one just question to ask the group and Mr. J .

"How was it possible for a ship to disappear?"

"It was a direct application of Einstein's Unified Field Theory which states that gravity and magnetism are connected, just as mass and energy are connected through Einstein's $E=MC^2$," Mr. J replied. "In fact, Einstein himself was there to make sure that we got it right."

In 1943, during the time that Mr. J had stated that the experiment in Philadelphia took place, Dr. Einstein was employed by the U.S. Navy as a scientific consultant, ostensibly for the Bureau of Ordnance. Records of the Office of the General Services Administration in St. Louis show that Einstein was employed intermittently in a Special Services Contract of the Department of the Navy, Washington, D.C. as a scientist from May 31, 1943, to June 30, 1944. Through those researches, I also found that the log of the *USS Eldridge* had been altered to say that it was not actually where it really was. Another researcher also discovered the logs of other nearby vessels which indicated that the *Eldridge* was present in Philadelphia.

When I went home after listening to Mr. J and his crew, my head reeled with new information. I have to admit, I was not sure about the information I had been given. I only knew that it was important.

11

BROOKHAVEN LABS

When I came home from school one day, my mother had a surprise in store for me. She said that Mr. J was going to pick me up on Saturday and take me on a "field trip." The next Saturday was a fall day in New York and a perfect day to go outside and practice some of the skills that I had learned in the Cub Scouts as I waited for Mr. J to pick me up. When he arrived at 9:30 a.m., he did not tell me where we were going. Once we started our trip, he made a nonchalant comment that he was taking me to BNL.

Arriving at BNL, Mr. J drove his car up to the guard shack at the entrance. Behind it was a 6 to 8 foot high chain link fence that was topped with barbed wire. There was also a three foot red brick wall with a white capstone located parallel to the chain link fence and the road. At the time, I had wondered what purpose the brick wall served. The facility already had a fence, and I assumed that it was just for decoration.*

The guard at the gate checked to see who was in the car. Mr. J then stepped out of the car and talked to the guard for a few minutes. I did not hear the whole

---

* Today, BNL has an "open" college-type campus and the chain link fence does not exist. However, the red brick wall is still there.

conversation, but Mr. J gestured towards me, and I assumed that that was what the conversation was about. When Mr. J got back into the car, we pulled away from the guard shack and headed towards the first building which was white and nondescript. I could not see any signs or numbers on it. On the way, Mr. J told me that we would encounter other guards and that he would have to stop and explain my presence. He said that the guard's name was Charlie and that if I ever wanted to get into the facility without him, I could. Mr. J ended by saying that I would get an identification badge later. It could not be done today because it was Saturday.

When we entered the building and were stopped by another guard, Mr. J again went through the process of introducing me and squared it away that I could go into the labs by myself. We next headed to the elevator. We were stopped again in front of the elevator by another guard. The introduction process was repeated once again with this guard. The elevator had two steel-mesh doors. The one on the inside was used by the occupants inside the elevator car. The other on the outside covered the entrance to the shaft. I had been in an elevator before in department stores, but this one was quite different. This made me so uncomfortable that when I went inside, I headed for the back of the car. Mr. J noticed my discomfort and suggested that I could use the stairs next time. On the way back, he would show me where they were. As we went down to the first subbasement, Mr. J hinted that there were more floors underneath. I asked him why the labs were underground, and he said it was to keep prying eyes away from their sensitive work.

As we got out of the elevator, another security guard was guarding the entrance to the floor. Mr. J yet again introduced me to the guard. We next walked down to the end of the hallway and entered the last laboratory door. The oak door was not labeled nor did it have any numbers stenciled on it. Mr. J said that this particular lab was concerned with the initial research of Project Rainbow. He went on to say that the part of Project Rainbow which dealt with the *Eldridge* was now known as the "Phoenix Project." He concluded by saying that this lab was only a small part of the Phoenix Project and that the project had spun off into many directions.

When we went inside the lab, I could see no difference between it and a chemistry lab you would see on TV or in the movies. The lab had rows of chemicals and chemistry apparatus complete with microscopes. These microscopes were what I was interested in. I received a toy microscope for Christmas, and I had spent countless hours looking at my prepared slides in it. Mr. J now gave me what he called "the big picture" of the developments of "Project Rainbow" and the "Phoenix Project." He now stated that the *Eldridge* had not really become invisible. It had been transported into hyperspace. Mr. J went on to say that the research on this phenomena continued with a series of steps. He and other scientists at BNL were trying to refine the experiment and control the phenomena. It was now twenty-five years after the initial experiment. Mr. J concluded by saying that this lab was only the beginning and an important cornerstone. The real work took place in the next room which was where the scientists realized what they were really working with.

12

THE CHAMBER

At the far corner of the lab was an ordinary looking oak door. We went through the door into the adjacent lab. Sitting in front of a keyboard and studying a video monitor, there was a technician dressed in a long white lab coat. On both sides of the walls around the keyboard operator, there were gray steel cabinets. The cabinets were divided into five panels, and each of the five panels contained six rows of five meters running horizontally. Underneath each meter was a big knob and below each knob was a toggle switch. Each meter and knob combination had labels such as "Discriminator Voltage," "Discriminator Amperage," "Discriminator Yield," "Detector Voltage," "Detector Amperage," "Peak Output," etc. These panels were quite unlike the banks upon banks of multicolored lights I had seen on TV or in the movies.

Mr. J explained that Project Rainbow had reached an initial stage. The experimental field had been reduced in size. At this stage of development, it had a twelve foot by twelve foot containment field. This reduction was very helpful and meant that the experiments could be conducted indoors. He continued to explain that these experiments were designed to help us develop navigational skills to explore hyperspace. Mr. J likened the experiments to those of the original explorers of the New World and that the researchers were akin to Christopher Columbus.

At the end of the room was a gray oval door which was opened to the inside. The door looked like a water-tight hatch you would find on a submarine. I walked up to the door and took a peek inside. Inside was the twelve foot by twelve foot room that Mr. J had spoken about. On the ceiling and on the floor was a ten foot square panel. Each panel was identical to the other. I walked back to Mr. J and asked him what it was for. He called it "the chamber" and said it was originally used for navigation, but it was now obsolete and used for transportation.

Mr. J said, "The chamber was used in the exploration of hyperspace. You see, hyperspace is but a doorway — a doorway into another dimension, one of time and space. It's amazing what you can learn once you've mastered time and space. Now, 'the chamber' is used to move men and equipment to where and when we want."

He continued to say that the original experiments opened the doorway. Once the doorway was opened, the researchers had to determine where it went and if it was safe. There were a lot of experiments to test for radiation, atmosphere, etc.

"Basically, we were stumbling around in the dark until we had a little help from our friends," Mr. J said. "The initial contact with our friends was established in 1918 when Nikola Tesla 'radioed' them on the planet Mars."

Mr. J explained that the sentient beings on Mars did not really live there but used the planet as their base of operations. He then continued.

"After the initial contact, Tesla developed a sub-space radio with which he talked to other extraterrestrials living in other galaxies. The language he used was mathematics."

Right then and there I was stupefied and almost fainted. President Kennedy had pledged to have a man on the moon before the decade was out, but now I was being told our government had spoken to extraterrestrials as early as 1918. This was 1968.

Did President Kennedy know? Or was it that he just was not told? Could it be that our government covered it up and announced that we would put a man on the moon just for window dressing? I could not get these thoughts out of my mind. Mr. J must have seen that I was upset by this revelation and decided that I had had enough. He said that we would go back upstairs now. We traced our steps back and went up the elevator. Before we left the building, Mr. J walked me over to a janitor's closet located at the other end of the ground floor hallway off to the left side of the lobby. The door was varnished oak and had a placard on it that said "Janitor's Closet."

As Mr. J opened the unlocked door and we went inside, I asked him why we were going in there. He did not answer. Inside were mops, brooms, and cleaning supplies. Mr. J went to the far corner where the mops and brooms were attached to hooks and pulled on the last unoccupied hook. The wall swung back revealing a room. Mr. J said that if we went through there, we would find a staircase leading down three levels. He also stated that it was not used very much because the staff preferred the elevator, but I could use it. Mr. J added that there were many floors underneath, but for security purposes they were not all connected by a single staircase. To get to the floors below the third floor, you had to find the other hidden staircases.

After hearing this last revelation, I just wanted to go home and think about it. Mr. J and I went back to his car and headed for home. On the way, he talked about the information he had shared with me and stated that there were only a handful of people in the country who knew about it. He said that even President Johnson (LBJ) did not know. According to Mr. J, LBJ did not want to know and left them alone.[*]

---

[*] After researching the MAJESTIC-12 documents in February of 2000, I could not find any reference that LBJ had ever been briefed on BNL. This could be either because he was never briefed or that the documents have yet to surface.

13

NIKOLA TESLA

Soon after visiting "the chamber," Dr. Stevens wrote another letter to me stating that he would like me to write to him care of a new post office box he had established. I subsequently informed him of what I had learned except for the part about my visit to BNL. I did not think it was wise to tell him about it just yet. I finished the letter to Dr. Stevens by telling him what Mr. J had said regarding Nikola Tesla and asked him to send me some background information on Tesla.

It took about ten days for me to receive a reply from Dr. Stevens. In the first part of his letter, Dr. Stevens explained that Nikola Tesla was born in Croatia (then part of Austria-Hungary) on July 9, 1856 and died January 7, 1943. Dr. Stevens said that Tesla was the electrical engineer who invented the AC (alternating current) induction motor which made possible the universal transmission and distribution of electricity. Dr. Stevens continued by mentioning that Tesla began his studies in physics and mathematics at Graz Polytechnic and then took philosophy at the University of Prague. He worked as an electrical engineer at Budapest, Hungary and subsequently in France and Germany. In 1888, Tesla discovered that a magnetic field could be made to rotate if two coils at right angles are supplied with AC current 90 degrees out of phase. This made possible the invention of the AC induction motor referred to above. Dr. Stevens concluded by saying that the major advantage of this motor was its brushless operation which many, prior to Tesla's successful invention of it, had believed was impossible. At the time, I did not understand what AC was let alone an AC induction motor. I did not even know what brushless was and had to look these terms up at the library.

In the second part of his letter, Dr. Stevens stated that Tesla moved to the United States in 1884 where he worked for Thomas Edison. The two quickly became rivals. For his own selfish monetary reasons, Edison advocated an inferior power transmission system that utilized DC (Direct Current). During this time, Tesla was commissioned with the design of AC generators installed at Niagra Falls. This turned out to be a huge success. George Westinghouse eventually purchased the patents to Tesla's induction motor and made it the basis of the Westinghouse power system. This still underlies the modern industrial power systems of today. After reviewing this last part of the letter, I had to look up who George Westinghouse was as well as DC power transmission. From movies on TV, I was already familiar with Thomas Edison and his work.

Dr. Stevens concluded his letter with the statement that Tesla did notable research on high-voltage electricity and wireless communication. At one point, he created an earthquake which shook the ground for several miles around his New York laboratory. He also devised a system which anticipated wireless communication, fax machines, radar, radio-guided missiles, and aircraft. When I read Dr. Stevens' letter in 1968, worldwide wireless communication, fax machines, radar, radio-guided missiles and aircraft were all in use in industry, the military, and police departments. Fax machines did not come into widespread public use until the 1980's. Either as an oversight or because it just wasn't that broadly known, Dr. Stevens did not mention Tesla's friendship with FDR.

After reading all this information from Dr. Stevens, it became very obvious to me that Tesla's research could easily have led to the experiments at the Philadelphia shipyard and beyond. The next part of the story, however, was a "gray" area for me. Three questions leapt into the forefront of my mind: (1) Who were these "friends" that Mr. J spoke of? (2) What kind of "exploration" was conducted at BNL? and (3) What did they find out on these "explorations?"

I decided to write another letter to Dr. Stevens and ask him point blank about Tesla's claim that he had communicated with extraterrestrials living on the planet Mars? After a week passed, I received a reply. In the letter, Dr. Stevens said that he had heard the rumor that Tesla had contacted beings outside of our own sphere of influence and that Tesla was laughed off by the established scientific community. Tesla was labeled "noncomposmentis" and not taken seriously.

Dr. Stevens' reply brought one question to mind. If Tesla was so brilliant then why was this claim about extraterrestrials laughed at? To me, he had more than proven his intelligence; therefore, any observation made by him had to have some merit. I was equally suspicious when Dr. Stevens ended his letter by saying that, at the time of Tesla's death in 1943, all of the inventor's research papers were seized for National Security purposes and put into storage in a government warehouse. Dr. Stevens did not elaborate on why this action was taken but only acknowledged that it took place. After having read Dr. Stevens' explanation, one very important question sprang to mind. If Tesla was truly insane, why were his papers seized? The Government could have easily displayed his papers and shown the public that he was insane, but they did not. Why? Although I have not seen Tesla's papers, I have talked to people who have, and they stated that they were quite brilliant and insightful.

Although it is not in the scope of this book to discuss Nikola Tesla's body of work, he played a valuable role in the development of the work being conducted at BNL. I hope to discuss the significance of Nikola Tesla's research in a later book.

14

MAJESTIC-12

In previous chapters I have mentioned MAJESTIC-12 and the documents associated with it. In this chapter, I will discuss my childhood recollections, what I learned about the crash at Roswell, the origin of MAJESTIC-12, and its influence on BNL. On the evening of July 7, 1947, there was a crash of an Unidentified Flying Object (UFO) near Roswell, New Mexico. This was not, of course, the first UFO to be spotted by the U.S. military. What was different about this case, however, was the vitality of this singular incident and the continuing developments in scientific, government, and legal circles that resulted.

According to the MAJESTIC-12 documents, the downed extraterrestrial craft near Roswell, New Mexico was either a wing or triangular shape. To the military, this type of craft had been seen before and was initially believed to be new technology from a foreign power. Radar indicated an isosceles triangle profile, the longest of these craft being nearly 300 feet in length. Little is known about the performance of these craft due to the rarity of good sightings, but they are believed to be capable of high speeds and abrupt maneuvers similar to or exceeding the performance attributed to elliptical and ovoid types. It is also thought that this type of craft is used primarily as a scout-ship capable only of achieving orbit.

At the time of the crash, there was not a single government agency concerned with the handling of these cases. OPERATION MAJESTIC-12 was established by special classified presidential order on September 24, 1947 at the recommendation of Secretary of Defense, James V. Forrestal, and Dr. Vannevar Bush, Chairman of the Joint Research and Development Board. Operations were carried out under a "TOP SECRET RESEARCH AND DEVELOPMENT" mandate. This intelligence group was directly responsible only to the President of the United States.

The following information regarding the activities of MAJESTIC-12 is taken from the MAJESTIC-12 GROUP SPECIAL OPERATIONS MANUAL dated April 1954.

"The goals of the MAJESTIC-12 (MJ-12) group are as follows: (a) The recovery for scientific study of all material and devices of a foreign or extraterrestrial manufacture that may become available. Such material and devices will be recovered by any and all means deemed necessary by the Group. (b) The recovery for scientific study of all entities and remains of entities not of terrestrial origin which may become available though independent action by those entities either by misfortune or military action. (c) The establishment and administration of Special Teams to accomplish the above operations. (d) The establishment and administration of secure facilities located at secret locations within the continental boarders of the United States for the receiving, processing, analysis, and scientific study of any and all material and entities classified as being of extraterrestrial origin by the Group of the Special Teams. (e) Establishment and administration of covert operations to be carried out in concert with Central Intelligence to effect recovery for the United States of extraterrestrial technology and entities which may come down inside the territory of or fall into the possession of foreign powers. (f) The establishment and maintenance of absolute TOP SECRECY concerning all the above operations.

MJ-12 took the subject of UFOs (Unidentified Flying Objects), Extraterrestrial Technology, and Extraterrestrial Biological Entities (EBE's) very seriously and considered the entire subject to be a matter of the very highest national security. For that reason, everything relating to the subject was assigned the very highest security classification."

Following is another excerpt from the MJ-12 documents headed under the designation "Current Situation."

"It is considered as far as the current situation is concerned, that there are few indications that these objects and their builders pose a direct threat to the security of the United States, despite the uncertainty as to their ultimate motives. Certainly the technology possessed by these beings far surpasses anything known to modern science, yet their presence here seems to be benign, and they appear to be avoiding contact with our species, at least for the present. Several alien cadavers have been recovered along with a substantial amount of

wreckage including devices or technological artifacts from the downed craft, all of which are now
under study at secure military/scientific locations.
No attempt has been made by extraterrestrial entities either to contact our authorities or to recover
their dead counterparts of the downed air craft,
even though one of the crashes was the result of
direct military action. The greatest threat at this
time arises from the acquisition and study of such
advanced technology by foreign powers unfriendly
to the United States. It is for this reason that the
recovery and study of this type of material by the
United States has been given such a high priority."

All information relating to MJ-12 has been classified
"MAJIC EYES ONLY" and carries a security level that is
two points above that of TOP SECRET. The reason for
this tight security has to do with the consequences that
may arise from the impact upon the general public should
the existence of such matters become general knowledge,
but also the danger of having such advanced technology as
has been recovered by the Air Force fall into the hands of
unfriendly foreign powers. No information is released to
the public press, and the official government position is
that no special group such as MJ-12 exists.

Eventually, the wrecked UFO and the dead occupants
from the Roswell crash (one of whom was reportedly alive
when found) were placed under high-security guard at the
Central Intelligence Agency (CIA) at Langley, Virginia.
MAJESTIC-12's job was that of enforcer. MJ-12 agents
bullied and coerced credible eyewitnesses of the crash at
Roswell into silence. Not until the 1980's did deathbed
confessions leak out about what really happened at Roswell,
New Mexico in 1947.

What the people running MAJESTIC-12 did not know was that there was another secret portion of the Government, even more secret than MJ-12, that had been talking to extraterrestrials for years and actually invited the EBE's here. It is a common misconception made by people researching the Roswell crash that the EBE's were simply interested in the developments of the atomic bomb at nearby Los Alamos. The reason the crash happened in the first place was that an unexpected bolt of lightning struck the craft. The occupants of the craft were on a reconnaissance mission to determine the level of development of atomic research conducted at Los Alamos, New Mexico. Through the communication Tesla had established with the EBE's, they were in the process of learning about our society, our strengths, our weaknesses, our obsessions, fears, and pathologies. As a species, they deemed us too primitive for them to take communication a step further than merely visiting us in person. But, when we successfully punched a hole into hyperspace (at the second experiment in Philadelphia), our status with them changed. This was the level of scientific achievement that continued to intrigue them.

According to my research, a society is put under the scrutiny of a galactic federation when it achieves a successful jump into hyperspace. The society is then evaluated for admission into this federation. They measure the society's intelligence and also its level of aggression towards others of its own and lesser species.

As of October 28, 1943, the U.S. was under surveillance from a distance to gauge its stability as a race. If our society is deemed too unstable for admission to the federation, steps are then taken to restrain and control our development. In other words, the EBE's were not interested in colliding atoms but rather the introduction of atomic weapons into hyperspace. You also have to understand that we were being watched during one of the century's bloodiest conflicts: World War II.

Newly discovered MAJIC-12 documents indicate that the Nazis had also seen the same type of craft recovered at Roswell. This would explain the rash of UFO sightings encountered by B-17 and B-24 crewmen over Germany during World War II. These UFO's were collectively known as "Foo Fighters."

Hyperspace is the conduit by which members of a galactic federation communicate and trade with each other. If an unstable society with atomic capabilities gained access to the hyperspace conduit, this would severely threaten the commerce and stability of the federation. This explains why there was a rash of UFO sightings in the 1950's in the United States. The EBE's were not spying on us to determine our use of atomic weapons but to access our maturity as a race.

The following pages contain what are popularly known as the MJ-12 documents. They were allegedly left under the home door of Hollywood producer Jaime Shandera by an unknown source in 1984. Stanton Friedman, a prominent and controversial UFO researcher, believes they are genuine based upon other documents found in the National Archives. Included is a briefing document put together for President Elect Dwight D. Eisenhower in 1952. It sheds light on what was going on in Washington, D.C. in the early 1950's. The EBE's were demonstrating their technological superiority in order to get the United States to negotiate a treaty with them.

These copies were the best I could find and had to be reduced a bit in order to fit into this size book so you might find reading glasses or a magnifying glass helpful. Please do not strain your eyes.

RESTRICTED

SOM 1-01
TO 12D1—3—11—1
MAJESTIC—12 GROUP SPECIAL OPERATIONS MANUAL

EXTRATERRESTRIAL
ENTITIES AND TECHNOLOGY,
RECOVERY AND DISPOSAL

TOP SECRET/MAJIC
EYES ONLY

WARNING! This is a TOP SECRET—MAJIC EYES ONLY document containing compartmentalized information essential to the national security of the United States. EYES ONLY ACCESS to the material herein is strictly limited to personnel possessing MAJIC—12 CLEARANCE LEVEL. Examination or use by unauthorized personnel is strictly forbidden and is punishable by federal law.

MAJESTIC—12 GROUP • *APRIL 1954*

MJ—12 4838B—Mar. 270480'—54—1

* TOP SECRET *
****

EYES ONLY   COPY ONE OF ONE.

On 24 June, 1947, a civilian pilot flying over the Cascade
Mountains in the State of Washington observed nine flying
disc-shaped aircraft traveling in formation at a high rate
of speed. Although this was not the first known sighting
of such objects, it was the first to gain widespread attention
in the public media. Hundreds of reports of sightings of
similar objects followed. Many of these came from highly
credible military and civilian sources. These reports resulted in independent efforts by several different elements
of the military to ascertain the nature and purpose of these
objects in the interests of national defense. A number of
witnesses were interviewed and there were several unsuccessful
attempts to utilize aircraft in efforts to pursue reported
discs in flight. Public reaction bordered on near hysteria
at times.

In spite of these efforts, little of substance was learned
about the objects until a local rancher reported that one
had crashed in a remote region of New Mexico located approximately seventy-five miles northwest of Roswell Army Air
Base (now Walker Field).

On 07 July, 1947, a secret operation was begun to assure
recovery of the wreckage of this object for scientific study.
During the course of this operation, aerial reconnaissance
discovered that four small human-like beings had apparently
ejected from the craft at some point before it exploded.
These had fallen to earth about two miles east of the wreckage
site. All four were dead and badly decomposed due to action
by predators and exposure to the elements during the approximately one week time period which had elapsed before their
discovery. A special scientific team took charge of removing
these bodies for study. (See Attachment "C".) The wreckage
of the craft was also removed to several different locations.
(See Attachment "B".) Civilian and military witnesses in
the area were debriefed, and news reporters were given the
effective cover story that the object had been a misguided
weather research balloon.

****
* TOP SECRET *
****

BRIEFING DOCUMENT: OPERATION MAJESTIC 12

PREPARED FOR PRESIDENT-ELECT DWIGHT D. EISENHOWER: (EYES ONLY)

18 NOVEMBER, 1952

<u>WARNING!</u> This is a TOP SECRET - EYES ONLY document containing
compartmentalized information essential to the national security
of the United States. EYES ONLY ACCESS to the material herein
is strictly limited to those possessing Majestic-12 clearance
level. Reproduction in any form or the taking of written or
mechanically transcribed notes is strictly forbidden.

****
* TOP SECRET *
TOP SECRET / MAJIC

T52-EXEMPT (5

EYES ONLY

EYES ONLY

83

SUBJECT: OPERATION MAJESTIC-12 PRELIMINARY BRIEFING FOR
    PRESIDENT-ELECT EISENHOWER.

DOCUMENT PREPARED 18 NOVEMBER, 1952.

BRIEFING OFFICER: ADM. ROSCOE H. HILLENKOETTER (MJ-1)

NOTE: This document has been prepared as a preliminary briefing
only. It should be regarded as introductory to a full operations
briefing intended to follow.

* * * * * *

OPERATION MAJESTIC-12 is a TOP SECRET Research and Development/
Intelligence operation responsible directly and only to the
President of the United States. Operations of the project are
carried out under control of the Majestic-12 (Majic-12) Group
which was established by special classified executive order of
President Truman on 24 September, 1947, upon recommendation by
Dr. Vannevar Bush and Secretary James Forrestal. (See Attachment
"A".) Members of the Majestic-12 Group were designated as follows:

        Adm. Roscoe H. Hillenkoetter
        Dr. Vannevar Bush
        Secy. James V. Forrestal*
        Gen. Nathan F. Twining
        Gen. Hoyt S. Vandenberg
        Dr. Detlev Bronk
        Dr. Jerome Hunsaker
        Mr. Sidney W. Souers
        Mr. Gordon Gray
        Dr. Donald Menzel
        Gen. Robert M. Montague
        Dr. Lloyd V. Berkner

The death of Secretary Forrestal on 22 May, 1949, created
a vacancy which remained unfilled until 01 August, 1950, upon
which date Gen. Walter B. Smith was designated as permanent
replacement.

COPY ONE OF ONE.

A covert analytical effort organized by Gen. Twining and
Dr. Bush acting on the direct orders of the President, resulted in a preliminary concensus (19 September, 1947) that
the disc was most likely a short range reconnaissance craft.
This conclusion was based for the most part on the craft's
size and the apparent lack of any identifiable provisioning.
(See Attachment "D".) A similar analysis of the four dead
occupants was arranged by Dr. Bronk. It was the tentative
conclusion of this group (30 November, 1947) that although
these creatures are human-like in appearance, the biological
and evolutionary processes responsible for their development
has apparently been quite different from those observed or
postulated in homo-sapiens. Dr. Bronk's team has suggested
the term "Extra-terrestrial Biological Entities", or "EBEs",
be adapted as the standard term of reference for these
creatures until such time as a more definitive designation
can be agreed upon.

Since it is virtually certain that these craft do not origin-
ate in any country on earth, considerable speculation has
centered around what their point of origin might be and how
they get here. Mars was and remains a possibility, although
some scientists, most notably Dr. Menzel, consider it more
likely that we are dealing with beings from another solar
system entirely.

Numerous examples of what appear to be a form of writing
were found in the wreckage. Efforts to decipher these have
remained largely unsuccessful. (See Attachment "E".)
Equally unsuccessful have been efforts to determine the
method of propulsion or the nature or method of transmission
of the power source involved. Research along these lines
has been complicated by the complete absence of identifiable
wings, propellers, jets, or other conventional methods of
propulsion and guidance, as well as a total lack of metallic
wiring, vacuum tubes, or similar recognizable electronic
components. (See Attachment "F".) It is assumed that the
propulsion unit was completely destroyed by the explosion
which caused the crash.

A need for as much additional information as possible about
these craft, their performance characteristics and their
purpose led to the undertaking known as U.S. Air Force Project
SIGN in December, 1947. In order to preserve security, liason
between SIGN and Majestic-12 was limited to two individuals
within the Intelligence Division of Air Materiel Command whose
role was to pass along certain types of information through
channels. SIGN evolved into Project GRUDGE in December, 1948.
The operation is currently being conducted under the code name
BLUE BOOK, with liason maintained through the Air Force officer
who is head of the project.

On 06 December, 1950, a second object, probably of similar
origin, impacted the earth at high speed in the El Indio -
Guerrero area of the Texas - Mexican boder after following
a long trajectory through the atmosphere. By the time a
search team arrived, what remained of the object had been almost
totally incinerated. Such material as could be recovered was
transported to the A.E.C. facility at Sandia, New Mexico, for
study.

Implications for the National Security are of continuing importance in that the motives and ultimate intentions of these
visitors remain completely unknown. In addition, a significant
upsurge in the surveillance activity of these craft beginning
in May and continuing through the autumn of this year has caused
considerable concern that new developments may be imminent.
It is for these reasons, as well as the obvious international
and technological considerations and the ultimate need to
avoid a public panic at all costs, that the Majestic-12 Group
remains of the unanimous opinion that imposition of the
strictest security precautions should continue without inter-
ruption into the new administration. At the same time, contingency plan MJ-1949-04P/78 (Top Secret - Eyes Only) should
be held in continued readiness should the need to make a
public announcement present itself. (See Attachment "G".)

··············
· TOP SECRET ·
··············

COPY ONE OF ONE.

ENUMERATION OF ATTACHMENTS:

*ATTACHMENT "A".........Special Classified Executive
                       Order #092447. (TS/EO)

*ATTACHMENT "B".........Operation Majestic-12 Status
                       Report #1, Part A. 30 NOV '47.
                       (TS-MAJIC/EO)

*ATTACHMENT "C".........Operation Majestic-12 Status
                       Report #1, Part B. 30 NOV '47.
                       (TS-MAJIC/EO)

*ATTACHMENT "D".........Operation Majestic-12 Preliminary
                       Analytical Report. 19 SEP '47.
                       (TS-MAJIC/EO)

*ATTACHMENT "E".........Operation Majestic-12 Blue Team
                       Report #5. 30 JUN '52.
                       (TS-MAJIC/EO)

*ATTACHMENT "F".........Operation Majestic-12 Status
                       Report #2. 31 JAN '48.
                       (TS-MAJIC/EO)

*ATTACHMENT "G".........Operation Majestic-12 Contingency
                       Plan MJ-1949-04P/78: 31 JAN '49.
                       (TS-MAJIC/EO)

*ATTACHMENT "H".........Operation Majestic-12, Maps and
                       Photographs Folio (Extractions).
                       (TS-MAJIC/EO)

87

15

MIND TAPPING

As my life unfolded, I pieced together the chain of events that led to the construction and eventual use of "the chamber" at BNL. The chronology is as follows:

1918 — Tesla contacts EBE's on Mars.

1918-1943 — Nikola Tesla works to realize and fullfil Albert Einstein's Unified Field Theory.

1942 — Dr. John von Neumann, director of Project Rainbow.

January 7, 1943 — Nikola Tesla found dead in his hotel room in New York.

July-October 1943 — tests on the *U.S.S. Eldridge* and others to create a ship that could not be detected by magnetic mines and/or radar.

October 28, 1943 — last experiment concluded on the *U.S.S. Eldridge*.

1946 — After the war, Project Rainbow, still under the tutelage of Dr. John von Neumann, is moved to BNL under the name "the Phoenix Project."

1955-present — Mr. J heads the Phoenix Project and supervises hyperspace/time travel experiments conducted at BNL until his retirement in 1978. This research eventually becomes the "Montauk Project."

After reviewing my notes as a kid, I realized that I still had a number of pertinent questions. Chief among them was "What explorations did the men at BNL conduct with 'the chamber?'"

I figured that the best way to find the answer was to ask Mr. J himself. I did not have to wait very long because the next get-together was that evening, and I was eager to find out what exactly "the chamber" at BNL was used for.

When I arrived at the house in Smithtown where the card game was held, I went straight to the basement where the men were busy playing. I was not even noticed as I walked into the room. Quietly, I padded over to Mr. J, unfolded a metal chair, and sat down next to him.

Mr. J nodded as he gave me a hello and whispered in my ear. He wanted to know if I had gotten over my experience at BNL. Stating that he had a lot more to show me, he said that I had only been exposed to the tip of the iceberg. When I let him know that I was up to seeing more, he said he would take me there again next Saturday.

At this point, I would like the reader to review the National Security Memorandum dated June 28, 1961 on the facing page. It has been transcribed more clearly below a scan of the original document. Also, please look at the draft of the memorandum dated November 12, 1963. It has also been transcribed on the next page. These documents were recovered from the National Archives.

When Saturday came, Mr. J picked me up in order to take me to BNL. On the way, he tapped his fingers on the black plastic steering wheel in time to the "swing" music coming from the car's AM radio speaker located on my

TOP SECRET   June 28, 1961

NATIONAL SECURITY MEMORANDUM

TO: The Director, Central Intelligence Agency.

SUBJECT: Review of MJ-12 Intelligence Operations as they relate to
Cold War Psychological Warfare Plans.

   I would like a brief summary from you at your earliest convenience.

TOP SECRET

                              Signed: John F. Kennedy.

Draft

TOP SECRET .

November 12, 1963

MEMORANDUM FOR
   The Director ███████████████, Central Intelligence Agency

SUBJECT: Classification review of all UFO intelligence files affecting
National Security

As I had discussed with you previously, I have initiated ████████████ and
have instructed James Webb to develop a program with the Soviet Union in
joint space and lunar exploration. It would be very helpful if you would have
the high threat cases reviewed with the purpose of identification of bona fide
as opposed to classified CIA and USAF sources. It is important that we
make a clear distinction between the knowns and unknowns in the event the
Soviets try to mistake our extended cooperation as a cover for intelligence
gathering of their defense and space programs.

When this data has been sorted out, I would like you to arrange a program
of data sharing with NASA where Unknowns are a factor. This will help NASA
mission directors in their defensive responsibilities.

I would like an interim report on the data review no later than February 1,
1964.

/S/ John F. Kennedy

92

TOP SECRET

November 13, 1963

MEMORANDUM FOR
   The Director (words crossed out) Central Intelligence Agency

SUBJECT: Classification review of all UFO intelligence files affecting National Security.

As I had discussed with you previously, I have initiated (words crossed out) and have instructed James Webb to develop a program with the Soviet Union in joint space and lunar exploration. It would be very helpful if you would have high threat cases reviewed with the purpose of identification of bona fide as opposed to classified CIA and USAF sources. It is important that we make a clear distinction between the knowns and unknowns in the event the Soviets try to mistake our extended cooperation as a cover for intelligence gathering of their defence and space programs.

When this data has been sorted out, I would like you to arrange a program of data sharing with NASA where unknowns are a factor. This will help NASA mission directors in their defensive responsibilities.

I would like an interim report on the data review no later than February 1, 1964.

John F. Kennedy

left and in front of me on the dashboard. I remained silent because I did not recognize the tune, but I could see that Mr. J really enjoyed it.

Arriving at BNL, we repeated our previous steps down towards the lab that housed "the chamber." This time, Mr. J led me across the hall to another oak door that was similar to and directly across the hall from the door we entered last time. He said that this room housed an "offshoot" of the chamber and was something they were not originally looking for. Mr. J concluded by saying that he had to tell me something before we went into the room and that was that "the chamber" opened the door to other applications that he found personally distasteful. It had to do with "mind control" experiments.

Mr. J said they had the ability to know what certain targets were thinking and that this could be determined from long distances away. He said that this was what the lab was used for. The only reason he showed it to me was because it explained why he had said "they would know if I told anyone." They could stop me because the device in there could read my thoughts. As we stood there in the doorway, I just wanted to run away and hide, but he looked down at me and told me not to be afraid and that it was all right. Mr. J then told me that this device was how he knew that I had talked to Dr. Stevens. They had read both of our minds and gave us the suggestion not to talk. I found this very difficult to believe. Up to that point, I believed everything Mr. J had told me, but this was a lot to swallow.

After 32 years, I have realized that I had not been able to tell anyone about this experience until now. Since that time, I always thought that the reason why I had never told anyone else about this was because I had given my word that I would not. After talking this over with Dr. Stevens, he said the same thing to me. Every time he wanted to tell someone about these matters, he could not. All he could think of was how much he would lose if he did.

Entering the "mind control" chamber, it looked the same as the lab across the hall, and I did not notice any differences. There was a keyboard, a monitor, and two cabinets of meters, knobs, and switches. It was then that I noticed the addition of two more cabinets with gauges and knobs and a placard at the top with the words written: "mind-transfer-interface."

Mr. J explained that it was basically the same lab but with additional equipment added to meets the needs of the experiment. He went on to say that they had found in their research that every person has an individualized "mind print" and to think of it like a "finger print." He said that this "mind print" was the same as the "soul." With this equipment, he said they could track someone down in time and space and know what they were thinking and influence their actions. Mr. J ended by saying that this project was funded by "the shop" and referred to as "the Phoenix Project." I asked him who "the shop" was, and he said it was a part of Central Intelligence interested in mind control and telekinesis. "The shop" wanted to use this machine to spy on the U.S.S.R. They already funded a remote viewing project, but this was cheaper and easier because anyone could do it, and it did not take someone gifted or trained as a remote viewer is. Mr. J ended by saying that the CIA did not know of the existence of the other chamber because they were not interested in time travel but only mind control. Consequently, they were never told about it.

The difference between the two labs was that the time travel lab had a chair in "the chamber." This chair was used by the remote viewer to see his target. The person seated in the chair had his "mind's eye" transferred to a different location such as the Soviet Union. Mr. J called the person sitting in the chair the "mindvoyager." The "mindvoyager" could then see structures and report (when the machine was switched off) on what he saw with his "mind's eye." He went on to say that this was cheaper than U-2's and spy satellites. Best of all was that anyone could do it, and the target did not know that it was being spied upon. Again, this was what he meant when he said that they would know if I told anyone. He also said that "the shop" already had a project in place for remote viewing in various universities across the country, but they did not use "the chair."

I have no idea how this machine worked or how any of their contraptions worked. My training in college has been in psychobiology — the study of how the brain and the mind interface. I have not been trained in theoretical physics even though I do have a basic understanding of physics and advanced mathematics. I make no claim of understanding the principles of the machinery that I have encountered. I do, however, know in fact that the fifty-one machines in question do indeed work. I only claim that the machines that Mr. J spoke of did what he said they did.

It is also important to address the issue of why I can talk about all this now. I feel that I was either switched back "on" to my recollections of the past or that the effects of the machine have simply worn off. I can offer no other explanation as to why I can speak of my experiences at BNL now. Perhaps the experiment was discontinued.

Although I find the mind control research (in the second lab) to be very distasteful, I feel that Central Intelligence, to some degree, may have been justified in its use. Today, people have a cloudy memory of the duck-and-cover bomb exercises we had to practice every week-day in elementary school. They also do not seem to remember how very close our country came to a nuclear exchange with the Soviet Union and the need for our country's leadership to be strong and at the same time secretive about our technological prowess.

After hearing all about this frightening technology on that particular day with Mr. J, I just wanted to go home, go to bed, go to sleep, and pretend this day never happened. Here I was, a little boy who was interested in a disappearing ship and now I had learned that part of the experiment was about controlling people's minds and spying. What would someone think if you went up to them and said that the Government has a machine that could control what you were thinking? They would probably think that the person saying this was nuts. Well, I was not nuts. I was just a kid who liked science but had suddenly become equipped with information that could turn the world upside down.

16

OVERLOAD

Being a precocious nine-year-old boy in the center of a cyclone was not an enticing prospect for me. I began to long for the day when my life was simpler and all I had to worry about was school. For a time, I decided to concentrate only on school and just move on with my life. Actually, this was a lot harder than it seems because even though I was upset by the latest developments, I wanted to learn more. I was deeply intrigued by the notion of seeing the past and finding out the answers to life's deep dark mysteries. I just never expected them to be handed to me on a silver platter. Eventually, I decided to tell Mr. J my feelings on the matter and asked him to tell me about the time travel experiments conducted in the first lab only. I thought that would soften the blow. After I became comfortable, I could move on to the rest of the data.

I did not have to wait long because Mr. J came to my house that night and told me the same thing. He apologized for his miscalculation of my reaction and said that he had made a mistake. Mr. J said that he did not have children and had treated me like an adult. He promised that in the future he would make an effort to keep that in mind when he talked to me. Even so, he said that he had other things to show me and ended by saying that this was even a lot for an adult to take in but that I had an open mind.

Next, Mr. J told me the overall scope of the project and how it began in the use of the chamber. Admitting that he had grown tired of all the cloak-and-dagger dramatics associated with his work, he said that in life you must take the good with the bad and insisted that his work was vitally important for National Security, but there were things out there more important than the petty squabbles that went with working for the Government. He thought that if I learned the good things that he did, I could, when the time was right, reveal them to the public. We both decided to go back and start over; this time taking it slow and easy. After all I was just a kid.

The following chapter is a synopsis of what I learned from Mr. J as well as what can be found in common research on Brookhaven National Laboratory. This includes BNL's origins during World War II and its official Nobel Prize winning research into the underlying structure of the atom.

17

AN OFFICIAL HISTORY

In 1946, when Norman Ramsey first visited the drab Army camp that had been selected as the location for a new atomic research laboratory, he was deeply disappointed. Ramsey, a Columbia University physicist who headed the site selection committee, knew the former Camp Upton would not appeal to the university scientists who would soon be recruited for the new laboratory near Yaphank, Long Island. With its muddy roads, wooden barracks, temporary shacks, and prisoner-of-war stockade, it was sterile and austere. At the suggestion of his wife, Ramsey compensated for these elements by choosing what he referred to as a "delightful misleading" name for the place: Brookhaven Laboratory. With its allusions to "quiet, shady, streams," he recalled later, the name "might make the laboratory site sound more attractive to potential new recruits than it actually was."

As it turns out, the site among the scrub oak and pitch pine soon was populated by hundreds of researchers more concerned about building a new research facility from scratch than they were about being comfortable. Many had ties to prestigious universities that had banded together to bring a government funded atomic research facility to the Northeast. These universities included MIT, Columbia, Cornell, and Princeton. Before World War II, Columbia University had been at the forefront of nuclear science. Experiments in the basement of the school's Pupin Hall led to the first artificial splitting of the atom on American soil. The Manhattan Project, the wartime effort to build the atomic bomb, was born in New York City; hence, the name. The Manhattan Project soon set up shop in Chicago, Illinois and then Los Alamos, New Mexico. Some Columbia stars, including Enrico Fermi and Harold Urey, moved west with the project and did not return.

Other wartime nuclear labs were established at Oak Ridge, Tennessee, and Berkeley, California. After the war, physicists in the New York area, who accounted for one-fifth of the members of the American Physical Society, realized that they had no world-class facility for studying the atom. I.I. Rabi, an eminent Columbia physicist, was particularly upset that his school's wartime contributions had led to a loss of faculty and facilities. Rabi was a driving force in the effort to persuade the Manhattan District of the Army Corps of Engineers (which ran the wartime A-bomb project) to establish a new peacetime lab in the New York region. When word spread to Boston, physicists from that area tried to lure the facility closer to their home campuses. Of the 17 sites initially proposed, all but the former Camp Upton near Yapank, in Suffolk County, Long Island proved unsuitable or unavailable. The executive committee for the new lab ratified Ramsey's proposed name on September 9, 1946. The contract officially creating Brookhaven National Laboratory was signed on January 31, 1947.

The war effort had shown that physicists, mathematicians, chemists, and other scientists could work together to accomplish goals not possible at a single university.

Brookhaven's founders hoped that their facility would show that such collaborations could work in peace time as well. In the early days, it was expected that people from all the departments would go to the combined colloquia in chemistry, physics, and biology. As the disciplines became more specialized, such general purpose meetings became impractical. But, the collegial spirit remained as the Brookhaven work force expanded rapidly during the 1950's. By the mid-1960's, there were 3,000 employees at the lab, and it had become a showcase for the construction of nuclear reactors, particle accelerators, and other frontier research machines that were too costly for individual universities to build. It also became a major employer and civic presence on Long Island. Few questioned this presence until recent years when a leak of radioactive tritium from the spent fuel pool of the lab's main reactor triggered community concern and questions by federal officials. This eventually led to the dismissal of Associated Universities, Inc., the contractor that had run the facility during its first half century.

Misgivings about Brookhaven have dogged the laboratory from the outset. According to Ramsey, the first complaint about radiation damage to outsiders occurred even before the site was officially occupied. After many months of disuse, the central heating plant at the former Camp Upton was started up, and smoke emerged from the chimney. A nearby resident called to complain that smoke from the laboratory's "atomic furnace" was aggravating her arthritis. As suburban growth enveloped the formerly isolated laboratory, Brookhaven's waste-disposal practices and day-to-day operations came under increased scrutiny by community activists and local officials. The laboratory's administrators and scientists now say they must pay as much attention to environmental quality as to the quality of the research being pursued. But, as Brookhaven struggles to regain the confidence of its neighbors, the laboratory's role in the history of American science seems secure. Brookhaven set the pattern for the development of other government-funded, multipurpose research laboratories. On an annual basis, over 2,400 scientists from across the nation and around the globe visit Brookhaven to use its research machines.

Brookhaven earned its original reputation in high-energy physics with studies carried out at the laboratory leading to four Nobel Prizes in physics. It has also become a repository for information on the design and safety of nuclear reactors. Additionally, the lab helped give birth to the field of nuclear medicine. Isotopes developed at the lab are now mainstays in the diagnosis and treatment of disease. In biology, laboratory scientists made fundamental discoveries about the effects of radiation on organisms and, more recently, have been helping to decode the human genome. Other scientists have developed advanced methods to image the working of the human brain.

Some of Brookhavens' research has exploited the labs's Long Island location. Brookhaven meteorologists track the Island's weather, oceanographers and biologists study its marine surroundings (including the brown tides that have devastated the Island's shellfish harvests), and biologists study the bacterium that causes Lyme disease, an affliction carried by deer ticks that was originally known as "Montauk Knee."

Brookhaven today is the fourth-largest high-tech employer on Long Island, with about 3,100 employees and 600 research programs. But, in the beginning, all of the electronic equipment at the laboratory could have been placed on a table top. The physics department consisted of five people. The library fit into two large bookcases.

By the summer of 1947, the lab was starting to grow rapidly. New staff members were arriving and plans were being made for the construction of a nuclear reactor on the highest hill on the laboratory's property, a promontory the physicists called Mt. Rutherford in honor of atomic pioneer Ernest Rutherford. The reactor, called the Brookhaven graphite research reactor, became operational in 1950 and served as one of the lab's primary research devices until it was decommissioned in 1968. It was the first U.S. reactor built solely for peaceful use.

Initially, the design of the graphite reactor was classified. Even though the research conducted with the device was not secret, scientists were required to have a security clearance to enter the building and to pass many security checkpoints once inside. This is the official rationale behind the extensive use of security resources for a non-secret research facility. Eventually, uncleared experimenters were allowed to use the west face of the reactor via a separate entrance. Access to the rest of the building was sealed off by a metal sheet dubbed the "iron curtain." Because of the presence of the new reactor, access to the Brookhaven grounds was carefully monitored in the early years with all visitors being stopped at the front gate. Today, there is still a guard at a booth who is backed up by a BNL security police force. The original chain-link fence is gone and the facility somewhat resembles a college campus.

Not everyone was in awe of the security procedures at Brookhaven. Maverick physicist and frequent visitor, Richard Feynman, was known for stepping on the accelerator when nearing the gate, speeding past the booth, sticking his head out of the window, and shouting at the startled guards, "It's all right, boys." Brookhaven's "iron curtain" was removed after the graphite reactor was declassified in 1955 as part of President Dwight D. Eisenhower's "Atoms for Peace" initiative. Eisenhower had toured the reactor construction site in 1948 when he was president of Columbia University.

While construction of the nuclear reactor was the primary reason for Brookhaven's creation, it was the particle accelerators that were to ensure its continued existence. The first was the Cosmotron, an accelerator used to send protons, at speeds approaching that of light, crashing into fixed targets. The resulting subatomic debris offered clues about the fundamental structure of matter.

The Brookhaven team raced to complete its Cosmotron machine before competitors at what is now the Lawrence Berkeley Laboratory in California finished a similar but larger device. The Brookhaven machine was completed in May, 1952 and became the first in the world

ATOMS FOR PEACE

Above is an award winning postage stamp rendered by Brookhaven Labs artist, George Cox, the father-in-law of Yoko Ono prior to her marriage to Beatle John Lennon. "Atoms for Peace" was a public relations initiative that sought to symbolize nuclear research as being for the collective good of all mankind. Somehow, after almost half a century, the idea still has not caught on in the public's mind.

to accelerate protons to an energy above one billion electron volts. In just five years, the laboratory in the middle of Long Island's pine barrens had become a top-ranked facility and a draw for physicists from around the world. Leland Haworth, the laboratory's director, began laying the groundwork for bigger things. In September, 1953, Haworth wrote a five page letter to the Atomic Energy Commission in Washington, D.C. outlining the rationale for what was to be the world's largest particle accelerator (or "atom smasher" as the popular press liked to call it). At the end of the letter, Haworth said simply, "I trust that the foregoing is sufficiently explanatory for your present purposes."

Within three months, Haworth received approval to build the device which was called the Alternating Gradient Synchrotron. It came on line in 1960 and for a dozen years was the nation's premier tool for exploring the microstructure of matter. Of course, the days when a five page letter could serve as the basis for funding a major research device are long gone. The final price tag for the device was $31 million dollars. In 1963, researchers used the synchrotron to discover two types of neutrinos. In the following year, they proved the violation of charge conjugation and parity which showed that the universe is not completely symmetrical. The J/psi particle, a key to proving the existence of quarks, was also discovered in 1964. All of these achievements were to win Nobel Prizes, but as newer and larger accelerators came on line, there were predictions that Brookhaven eventually would be eclipsed. Competing efforts were at the Fermi National Accelerator Laboratory near Chicago, Illinois and also at a laboratory near Geneva, Switzerland.

An effort to build the next-generation colliding beam accelerator (initially called Project Isabelle) at Brookhaven was canceled in 1983 after technical problems arose concerning the huge magnets to be used in the device. The 2.4 mile long circular tunnel that had been built for the device sat empty. Despite this major setback, Brookhaven rebounded. Lab officials proposed another research device for the ring dug for Isabelle. It is called the RHIC which stands for Relativistic Heavy Ion Collider. This new machine, which is scheduled to go on line as the book you are reading is published, will send clusters of atomic nuclei crashing into each other to create a super hot plasma that is designed to mimic conditions in the universe during the first moments after the Big Bang.

A half century after its founding, Brookhaven is on the verge of recapturing some of the excitement and intellectual fervor that goes with the inauguration of a front-ranked research device. But, the ferment beyond the front gate cannot be ignored either. By this, I am referring to the secret activities that have occurred there since its inception. What I have stated in this chapter is the official history of Brookhaven National Laboratory. There is also an unofficial history.

Unbeknownst to the dedicated Nobel Prize winning scientists, the data collected from their projects was shuttled to Dr. John von Neumann's team working on "The Phoenix Project" located in the subbasements at Brookhaven National Laboratory. Brookhaven is at the forefront of science, and it also is at the forefront of a number of issues relating to the use of alien technologies and their effects on human society. How it handles those issues is going to be important for us all. This relationship will be expanded and discussed in the rest of this book.

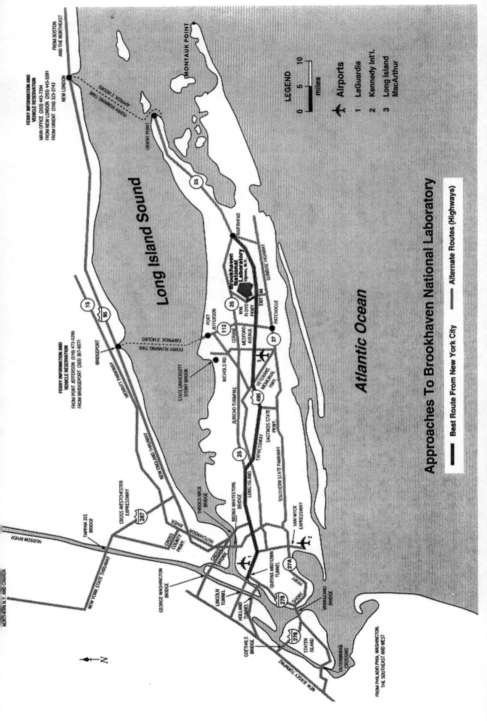

Approaches To Brookhaven National Laboratory

■ Best Route From New York City   ━━ Alternate Routes (Highways)

109

18

AN UNOFFICIAL HISTORY

Eager to learn more about "the chamber," I was hesitant to learn anymore about mind control for the time being. It was not that I did not want to know. I was just a little boy who snuck into card games. I was not ready to learn more, and I knew that I could not handle the information. I figured that in time, once I got used to the idea, I would be ready to learn more about mind control and its implications in our society.

When Mr. J visited me, he told me that he had come to the same conclusion as me and decided that he should slow down. In fact, he told me that the reason he came by was to see how I was holding up under the strain. He mentioned that he knew a few adults that had the same information that I did and could not handle it. Mr. J asked me for the second time whether he should stop altogether or continue at a much slower pace. In no uncertain terms, I told him that it was not an easy decision to make. I wanted to continue but first wanted to take a short break for a few weeks to clear my head and regain my focus. He agreed to my solution and said that he would "get in touch" with me in two weeks. The two weeks came and went by very fast. The next thing I knew, my mother announced

111

that there was going to be another "get-together" in East Islip that night. It was the beginning of November, and my head was preoccupied with football. I was beginning to get excited about the upcoming holidays and the thought of "the chamber" never entered my mind.

The house we went to in East Islip was the same one that I had gone to previously. When I met with Mr. J and the other men, I told them I was not very excited about learning more about BNL. Mr. J formally apologized to me again, but this time in front of his men. I was very impressed by his integrity.

As Mr. J and the men talked, they discussed the official work going on at BNL and said that this work would probably earn at least one Nobel Prize. Before I could think about what I said, I blurted out this was unfair and said time travel and the chamber were more important than the atom. Why didn't Mr. J and his team earn a Nobel Prize for that? I ended by saying that they deserved it.

I really should have thought those last statements out because what little excitement that was in the room suddenly died down. The room became quiet and pensive until Mr. J noticed the mood and spoke up. He thanked me for my support but said that the "big shots" in Washington did not want any publicity over what they were doing. He said they were all well compensated for their discretion and that the money did not matter. It was very exciting work and they were lucky to be paid for what they loved to do. The only hitch was that they could not tell anyone and that was why I was here. My job was to tell others of the "big picture" that they were working on. Mr. J finished by saying that this was a sensitive area in their work and that I was to not to bring it up ever again.

Waiting a few moments before answering, I said that I agreed with his plan of action. I next asked Mr. J and the men to explain the events that happened after the ship (the *U.S.S. Eldridge*) disappeared in Philadelphia and after the program was moved to BNL. Mr. J replied by saying that when the vessel disappeared, the men on the ship experienced horrible side effects. The Navy did not know exactly what had happened. They knew that they had something of great importance, but they did not know exactly what to do with it. And, more importantly, there was the question of how could they apply what they had learned to the defense of the country.

When the Philadelphia Experiment research was moved to BNL, Mr. J said he began to work on it. He said that he had been working at Columbia University when he received a letter asking him to appear for an interview. At first, he did not know what the project entailed, but after discussing it with superiors in his department, he decided to give it a shot. Mr. J was told that it was very secret work and that he would be very well paid for his research. What he found out at the interview was that they were looking for "fresh blood" to investigate a very interesting experiment. Dr. John von Neumann had interviewed him and was very impressed with his "take charge" personality and knew that he was the right man for the job. Although Mr. J was intrigued with the opportunity, he still did not know exactly what they were working on. He was also very impressed when Dr. von Neumann had said that Einstein had been working on the program but left because he did not think that the project should be under military control. Mr. J knew Einstein and had talked to him personally about the project. According to Mr. J, he said that Einstein did not want any part of it and wished that it would just go away. Even so, Einstein added that he felt that Mr. J was the right man for this job. Mr. J went on to say that the project was classified above "TOP SECRET," all reports were to be "EYES ONLY," and that no copies were to be made of the documents. He said that this was a "Black Project" and that there were no records of its existence.

When Mr. J came aboard the project, his job was to oversee the observation and study of the properties that the experiment exhibited, design tests for further studies, and report his findings directly to Dr. von Neumann. Mr. J stressed that the U.S. was still embroiled in World War II and that the Navy was especially interested in any project that could be used to shorten the war. He also went on to say that, because of the nature of the work, the Navy was looking for single men to work on the project because married men were likely to tell their spouses. Mr. J said that that was no longer the case because most of the men working with him were on his original team and were all happily married and never said a word to their wives. At least, that is what they told him. He trusted their integrity and knew that no member of his team would ever talk. To that date, he and his men, with a few additions, had been working on the project for over twenty-one years without any known security leaks.

Mr. J continued his history lesson by saying that he and his men designed a series of experiments to find out what exactly happened when an object disappeared. Probes were built to test for radiation and atmosphere, and this went on for about a year. He said that because of their funding and the designation of the project, the Government was not interested in weekly and monthly reports. All he had to do was meet with Dr. von Neumann to discuss their findings and agree to the next step. It was a careful and methodical process because they were exploring uncharted territory and did not know what exactly the consequences of their actions would be. Because of the unknown dangers involved in the research, Mr. J and his team had to have weekly physical examinations to gauge their body's reactions to the exposure of radiation. After about a year, the physical exams tapered off to a monthly exam and then a six month exam. The results of their probes showed that there was no atmosphere in hyperspace but that there were significant radiation readings. Mr. J likened the radiation to the radiation found in the Van Allen* belts that surround the earth.

Mr. J.'s team surmised that if precautions were taken such as pressure suits and radiation shielding, men could be sent into hyperspace safely. These tests were initially funded by the Navy; but, with the tide of the war changing and the Allies winning the war, the Navy lost interest and was thinking about cancelling the project. This all changed by the summer of 1947 with the "crash" at Roswell, New Mexico. By 1947, the Navy all but cancelled the funding, but in that same year, MAJESTIC-12 was created by presidential directive and took over the program at BNL. Mr. J said that this was when the direction of the project changed. Up to that time, all they had been doing was trying to find out where hyperspace led to; however, the men at MAJESTIC-12 already knew about hyperspace. This revelation shocked Mr. J because he thought that his team's work was above TOP SECRET. But, these men knew of their existence. According to Mr. J, in the initial briefing he had with MAJESTIC-12, one of the survivors of the crashed craft had told them of Mr. J's work. This was another shock to him, but the shock was not about the crash. Mr. J said that with all the millions upon millions of stars in the heavens, there must be some intelligence out there greater than ours. It was only logical to come to this

---

* Van Allen belt: Either of the two broad bands of intense radiation in outer space that surround the earth, consisting of charged particles which are apparently held by Earth's magnetic field. The belts are named after the American physicist James A. Van Allen who discovered them in 1958.

conclusion. What shocked him was learning of an agency more secret than his that had an EBE who told them of his work. It seems that every time hyperspace is opened up, it shows up on the EBE's instruments. In this case, they had come to investigate our progress. Mr. J confessed that this was something he never dreamed he would ever hear. How could a portion of our government, much less an alien life form, know of their work? Needless to say, after the initial shock wore off and he got used to the idea, it did not seem all that hard to believe.

At this historic meeting with MJ-12, Mr. J said the men claimed they had been given a directive from the EBE's to change the project. The EBE's wanted us to experiment in time. This was something Mr. J had never dreamed of: time travel. How could that be possible? Later, I was told that Mr. J had been given a set of directions on how to make time travel possible. This was something that he and his team did not even know was possible. According to the directions supplied by the EBE's, his team had to build extra equipment to add to the existing structures and instruments. This would ensure travel in time. Most importantly, he was given directions on how to make the containment field smaller so that matters could be handled in a small room. Mr. J said that they were only able to make so much progress in so short a time because they had help. The experiments suddenly had a direction: the investigation of time travel.

When I heard this last bit of information from Mr. J, it hit me with the force of revelation. The United States was experimenting with time travel and it was not the stuff I saw in movies or television; but, the U.S. had help. I then asked Mr. J why the EBE's had offered to help us in the first place, but he waved off this question and said that all of my inquiries would be answered "in due time."

The first thing I needed to learn was what "time" really is. Mr. J explained that to a "normal" person, time flow is linear and only in one direction and that people of different ages experience time differently. He said that this was accounted for by the fact that at different times in life, our brain chemistry is different; hence, our perception of time is different. "Time," Mr. J said, "is like a piece of string; hence, the name "String Theory."

He said, "If you take a piece of string and roll it into a ball, you can then go from point to point in a person's lifetime. And, with the right equipment and a lot of practice, you can jump around very easily."

I found this concept very hard to grasp. After some time, Mr. J admitted to me that he and his team had felt the same way, too. How could time be made into a string? We cannot even see time but can only sense its passing. He said that you have to think of time in the same way that you think of light. Light is really particles in wave action. That is why light exhibits particles and wave characteristics. Time is essentially the same thing but on a different frequency. This also explains why certain prophets can transcend time through meditation. Mr. J said that these people can change their brain chemistry and thus their perception of time.

Mr. J said that a philosopher/scientist named Jacob Brownowski understood this concept of time. He said that Brownowski had written a most thought provoking book on this subject entitled *Science And Human Values*. Later, Mr. J gave me a copy of the book with a particular quotation marked that said, "Reality is not an exhibit for man's inspection, labeled 'Do not touch.'"

There are no appearances to be photographed and no experiences to be copied in which we do not take part. Science, like art, is not a copy of nature but a recreation of her. We remake nature by the act of discovery whether it be in a poem or in a theorem. The great poem and the deep theorem are new to every reader and are his own experiences because he himself recreates them. They are the marks of unity in variety; and, in the instant when the mind seizes this for itself, in art or in science, the heart misses a beat.

It was not until 1977 that I understood Brownowski's views. At that time, I was an undergraduate attending New College at Hofstra University and the aforementioned book was on the book list for a humanities class. It was also at this point that I met the author Paddy Chayefsky who was researching his book *Altered States* which was eventually made into a movie of the same name released in 1979. Mr. Chayefsky's novel and subsequent movie was loosely based on the life of scientist/philosopher John C. Lilly who started experimenting with isolation tanks in 1954. Mr. Lilly's most notable book was *Center of the Cyclone* published in 1972. Mr. Chayefsky and I spent many an autumn afternoon sitting in Hofstra's rathskeller drinking Canadian Ale and discussing the finer points of his research into altered states of consciousness. When he noticed that I was carrying Jacob Brownowski's *Science And Human Values*, a spirited discussion of the book ensued. At the time, I was studying psychobiology; more specifically, the subject of how music influences mind/brain development. Today this theory is called "The Mozart Effect."

19

TIME

Mr. J had said that time was like a string; and if you wound it up, you could jump from point-to-point. Well, that was very hard for me to understand. The first question that popped into my mind was, "How do you wind it up?"

This is what went through my mind when I got home that night. First, I wanted to know how you see time as a string in order to wind it up. I decided right then and there that this information was way over my head. I was at the card games to learn about BNL research, not understand it. I could make myself crazy obsessing about it. Besides, it was football season, and to a scrappy kid, this was the most important thing in my universe. What did I care about time? When you are a kid, you think you have all the time in the world.

Before I left the card game one night, Mr. J mentioned that he would tell me later why the EBE's were interested in helping us explore time. This was exciting, and I could hardly wait until I saw him again to ask him my questions about time as a string. Before this train of thought evaporated, I decided to sit down and write Dr. Stevens a letter and tell him what I had learned about time. I did not think he knew about it already, and I thought he would like to hear it. Deciding to put it as bluntly as I could, I told Dr. Stevens that Mr. J said that time was like a string. Having no knowledge about what his reaction might be, I finished the letter, put it in an addressed stamped envelope, and mailed it to Dr. Stevens.

My next project was to go to the library and find out all I could about time. When I got to the East Islip Public Library, I walked up to the reference desk and asked the librarian to help me find books about time. What the reference librarian gave me was a copy of *Time* magazine. It was definitely not what I wanted. When I politely told her this, she insisted that the philosophical books dealing with the concept of time were not for me. She said that I would not be able to understand all the big words in it and asked me if there was anything else she could help me with. When I did not answer her, she walked away from me. I had run up against a thing that I could not control: my age.

I was still very young and was not taken seriously. I had only two options: to see Mr. J again or wait for Dr. Steven's reply to my letter. With this question gnawing away at my brain, I decided to ask my mother's permission to call Mr. J and ask him about it. She gave me permission and dialed his number that same evening. When I told him about what had happened in the library, he chuckled. After he finished chuckling, he told me that the librarian did not understand the question and that it was not my fault. Mr. J said that most people do not understand the concept of time; they just experience it. He told me not to worry about it and that when I was ready to understand the concept, it would come to me.

I felt he was answering me with a riddle and got a little angry as I defensively barked, "You're just like her. You think that I'm a little brat whose britches are too big."

Mr. J then told me to calm down and that was not the point. It was just that my brain had not matured enough to understand the concept of time and that I eventually would. He said that even the great Einstein did not fully understand the concept of time even though his paper of 1905 entitled "The Electrodynamics of Moving Bodies" predicted time displacement. Mr. J ended by saying that Einstein said in his "Theory of Relativity" that relativity is the understanding of the world not as events but as relations. And, when you are ready to understand this starting point, you can then move on and understand the string theory of time. Before we ended our brief phone conversation, Mr. J reminded me to be patient and that in time I would understand what he was trying to tell me. It was a good thing that we ended the call because I was beginning to think he was patronizing me.

After some time, I cooled off. I began to see the method in the madness. I was learning about something I could not see but only experience. That was the point that all the philosophers were trying to make. Time was not something you could see, taste, or feel. It was something you could only experience. But, how can you control something you can only experience? This I would learn in a short time. I would learn that they could control it, but I could not understand how they did it. Slowly, a picture began to resolve itself in my mind. I began to see what really happened at BNL. I began to see through the clouds of blue smoke created to mask what was taking place at BNL from prying eyes. Suddenly, I knew what the explorers of the New World must have felt. Their eyes were open to accept life's great mysteries. I could not wait for the next "get-together" so that I could learn more.

20

AN E.B.E. CONNECTION

What I liked about Islip Terrace was that it was a "garden spot." It had the feel of what Long Island used to be like before the intrusion of the suburbs. This part of the Town of Islip was an agricultural community until, one by one, the small farms "sold out" to the land developers. This part of Islip Terrace still felt like country living. At heart, I guess I am a country boy who does not like being surrounded by concrete.

When I arrived in Islip Terrace for the next card game, I headed straight for the basement. I was no longer timid or insecure about my place in the group. Finding the basement door on the opposite side of the staircase to the second floor, I walked down the flight of wooden steps that led to the concrete floor where the basement had been turned into a family room with wood paneling and a plush carpet. The room was well-lighted and I could see a dart board on one of the paneled walls. The men, occupied in their card game, were discussing sports. It was football season and the men were talking about the state of the New York Giants' defensive team. I really had no interest in the Giants, but I liked the Miami Dolphins and the New York Jets. I was especially interested in the progress of Joe

Namath, the Jets' new quarterback. I never dreamed that I would ever hear these scientists discussing the strengths and weaknesses of a football team. In fact, I did not even know that these men liked sports at all.

When the men noticed me, they stopped talking and all said hello. I really was welcome in their group, and their kind greetings made me feel a lot more comfortable about joining them. Mr. J had not arrived yet, but the men had told me that he was on his way. We did not have to wait too long until Mr. J showed up and joined the group. He was in a very good mood and hummed while he came down the stairs and gregariously greeted all of us. Unable to wait for him to join us at the table, I quickly walked to the bottom of the stairs and met him. Saying hello, I quickly asked him to explain to me again what exactly time was, but he said it could wait until he got to the table.

When Mr. J got to the table, he handed an envelope to each one of the men that were present. He told them that this was the "extra" he promised and instructed them not to tell their wives about it. Not knowing what he was talking about, I assumed that it was money. He then sat down and announced that I could not even wait for him to even sit down before asking him about time.

"Could anyone here present help this young man out?" Mr. J asked the men with a rascally smile.

One of the men at the card game spoke up and asked, "What exactly does the young man want to know?"

"If you can't see, feel, or touch time, how do you know that it's there?" I asked.

"Well," he replied. "Let me put it into terms that you would understand. Don't get defensive. I'm not implying that you're dumb or anything of that nature. What I mean to say is, time is really a form of energy vibrating at a specific frequency. If you find out what the frequency is, you can tap into it and manipulate it."

"You mean," I replied, "you can find the frequency of time and get into it? It's just that easy?"

"Well, it really wasn't that easy and took us over ten years just to work that part out. It was a long and arduous task. We were given a set of instructions on how to do it, but that was easier said than done."

"Who gave you the set of instructions?" I asked.

"It was a representative of the Galactic Federation, or for want of a better term, an EBE. An EBE gave us the plans but didn't tell us how to follow them. The plans were a mathematical formula with a primer at the top of the page."

"Why didn't the EBE show you how to do it?"

"We found out later that it was a test. A test to see how intelligent we were, but to be more specific, it was a test to see how diligent we were."

"I take it that you passed the test."

"Well, we did have some glitches and minor setbacks which was to be expected when working with such an intricate problem."

"What did the EBE look like?"

"That is a rather difficult question to answer. The EBE's recovered in the crash at Roswell could be described as Chinese dwarfs. These were not really the representatives of the Galactic Federation. Actually, they were drones. Drones that were trained to operate the craft. In fact, you might say that they were created for just that purpose. These drones were made from a genetic template and are more commonly referred to as clones. The same principle used to create them has been used for centuries in botany. These clones were specifically designed to operate the craft in space. They just operated the craft and did not make decisions. That was left up to their superiors."

Mr. J then interrupted our conversation and said that was enough of that line of inquiry. The man who had been speaking then suddenly interrupted Mr. J and added that he would like to finish his point. Mr. J said that it was all right for him to finish.

"The surviving drone from the crash at Roswell instructed his captors (the U.S. Army) how to contact its superiors. The Army did and this is how we eventually learned who they were and how we were given a set of instructions on how to travel in time.

"What we found out is that everything, and I mean everything, vibrates or has a frequency — and that includes atoms."

Mr. J added, "But enough of this discussion. What you wanted to learn about was time. Time has very unique properties — properties which my team has only begun to unravel and we've been at it for a very long time. I think it is only fitting that I show you what we've been talking about. Next Saturday, I will take you down to the lab that contains the answers to your questions."

Mr. J did not broach this subject again for the entire evening. The men just continued to play cards. As I sat there, I imagined what he was going to show me in that lab.

21

UNDISCOVERED COUNTRY

Mr. J showed up the very next Saturday to take me to BNL and the subbasement lab once again. This time, he was very quiet and did not even hum along to the swing music playing on the car radio. When we arrived at BNL and went through the usual check points, the guards knew who I was and did not bother to check us and just waved us on.

As we made our way down in the elevator with the steel mesh inner door, Mr. J said that in two weeks the lab would be busy hiding its existence. Asking him what he meant by that, he replied that a congressional delegation was coming by to inspect the graphite reactor. He said that these congressmen were coming by for a photo-opportunity and press conference to announce the construction of a new reactor to replace the one already in existence. The official reason, Mr. J added, was that the reactor had served its purpose and needed to be replaced. These congressmen were coming by for the ribbon cutting ceremony for the new reactor. Mr. J said that this was really just a big public relations gimmick because the reactor did not actually need to be replaced. What was really happening was that the contractor used for the construction of the new reactor was a heavy contributor to these congressmen's reelection committees and the congressmen were just returning a political favor. Mr. J said that it had something to do with "pork barrel politics."

As we made our way down to the first subbasement and walked down the hallway, Mr. J said that there were a couple of things he would like to clarify before we entered the next lab. He said that because of the congressional delegation's visit, he and his group were given two weeks off. He said that this was S.O.P. (standard operating procedure) when "big shots" toured the lab. This was just a photo-opportunity to validate the continuation of the "Atoms for Peace" initiative. All of the "ABOVE TOP SECRET" programs were closed down and the men were sent home. He said that this was good because it gave him and his men a needed break. Although they used this time to "get to know" their families again, it was also important for the work. The R&R (rest and relaxation) gave him and his team the opportunity to rethink the work ahead.

Stopping in front of a door that I had never noticed before, Mr. J said that I should mentally prepare myself before I entered. He called this "The Undiscovered Country," admitting that he borrowed this term from William Shakespeare, but I did not even know who William Shakespeare was at that time. Mr. J said that he had wanted to put a sign above the door with a quote from Dante's Inferno that read, "Abandon all ye hope before you enter here" but decided that was too dark and cynical. Again, I had no idea just what he was talking about. He next said that he had decided instead to put up a sign that read "The Undiscovered Country" because he felt that was a better description of the work that they conducted there. I made a mental note to go to the library to look up Dante and Shakespeare. The final thing he said before we went in was that this lab was a "refinement" of the chamber based upon the inclusion of data supplied by the "supervisor" of the occupant of the craft that crashed at Roswell, New Mexico.

Entering the lab, Mr. J reached over, flicked the wall switch, and turned on the overhead lights to the lab. Unable to see any difference between this lab and the ones we had been in previously, I wondered if Mr. J was joking with me or trying to scare me with that information he had given me before we entered. The only thing I noticed different about this lab was that there were a lot more gray panels of knobs, switches, and meters than there had been in the other two labs.

When Mr. J spoke up, he said that before they could travel in time, they had to pinpoint specific targets. To do this, he explained, they needed to find a way to "lock-on" to the target in question. With the data supplied by the EBE, and after a lot of years of exhaustive trial and error, they succeeded in finding a target within the chamber. He added that while they were experimenting with the data for the chamber, everyone on the team had a sneaking suspicion that this might be some sort of trap and not the road to enlightenment. But, after a few years of experimentation, everyone on the team began to feel that their suspicions were unfounded and just "Cold War" paranoia. What they discovered was that these EBE's really wanted to help us, but first, we had to prove worthy of their help by solving their riddle and making the chamber work.

When I asked Mr. J how they were able to find a target, he said they discovered this after painstakingly deciphering an alien template. The instructions indicated that a subject in the chamber would be able to travel backward in his own lifetime by directing the use of the subject's "mind print" in direct application with "the

String Theory." The subject's body stayed in the chamber while his "mind pattern" changed places with its past counterpart. The present was in the past, while the past was in the present. Both the subject and the target remained conscious while the procedure was carried out. When the process was reversed, both "mind prints" returned to their initial states. The subject in the chamber had full recollection of what had transpired. Mr. J then said that when the transference had taken place, the target in the chamber was interviewed to find the date of the transference.

At this point in Mr. J's explanation, I stopped him to clarify a point. I wanted to repeat to him what he had said in order to make sure that I got the information correctly. I said that the data supplied by the EBE's was used to refine the chamber and his team had discovered that it was possible to travel in time. The team used a subject in the chamber; and, after further testing, they were able to control how far back in the subject's lifetime they went.

When I asked him what use would such a device be, Mr. J answered with a riddle, "What is the use of a newborn baby?"

Mr. J continued to say that it could be used to observe past events if they were able to direct the target's actions through the use of the subject. He confessed that in the first experiments this was not possible and the subject merely reacted to events without any prior knowledge or guidance supplied by the future. That was only the first major step in their research and was not reflective of their current capabilities. At the time, his team as well as his superiors were satisfied with the results; but soon, his superiors put pressure on him and his team to take the project to the next level and influence the past. They were very eager to exploit that faint possibility.

I asked Mr. J if he thought the EBE's would be happy if his team were able to influence the past. After careful consideration of the problem, he said that he came to the conclusion that this was the ultimate goal of the test: to see if mankind was mature enough to handle the temptation and not seek the short term political benefits with the use of such power. This is the viewpoint he tried to convince his superiors with. He confessed that his superiors were a "tough sell" and stressed a major point to them: if the EBE's had the power to accomplish this, think of the things that they themselves would in turn be able to accomplish. In the end, they would come out ahead if they acted responsibly. And, if he and his team successfully passed the test, the EBE's would give them more information that might be used to alleviate pain and suffering and provide cures for crippling diseases as well as supplying needed information to solve some of the great unsolved mysteries in the history of man. Mr. J ended by saying that he was surprised at his superiors reaction to his proposal and that in his words, "It took a lot of wrangling for them to see the big picture."

In the end, his superiors kept the status quo and the team continued their cautious approach. Mr. J confessed that he was satisfied with that. He said that he had one trick up his sleeve that ensured the survival of his team and their project. In their research up to that point, there had been indications of an imminent breakthrough. Soon, the team would be able to target anywhere in a subject's lifetime, past or future. This would enable them to have the subject "remember" the future and use this information in the past. Mr. J went on to say that he had used at least one test in particular that proved to his superiors that he was on "the right track" and ensured the funding and continuation of his team for years to come.

In the early months of 1964, his team took a rather bold maneuver. At that time, the country was still reeling from the effects of the Kennedy assassination. His plan was to send a subject back to Dallas a few days before the assassination and bring back conclusive evidence of what really happened on November 22nd, 1963.

When I asked Mr. J how he was able to do this, he said the answer had leaped out of his brain. He would send a man back and place him in the area with the specific instructions only to observe because he felt the EBE's wanted us to be observers only and not upset the delicate time stream. Asking him how he was able to provide direct proof if they could not bring anything back, he answered that this was the beauty of the idea: send a man back, tell him to get a camera with a telephoto lens, take a picture of the action, and put the film in a bus terminal locker. He admitted that this was not as easy as it sounded. There were a lot of logistical problems such as finding a locker, making a duplicate key, and finding a way for the subject to contact the team in order to come back to the present. Nevertheless, they went ahead with the plan to bring back information from November 1963 to February 1964.

22

NOVEMBER 1963

The following is my account of the big experiment that Mr. J related to me that his team conducted in order to demonstrate to "the powers that be" what he and his team were capable of accomplishing.

It was the second week of February in 1964, and the entire country was in turmoil about the assassination of President Kennedy. Mr. J wanted "something big" to convince his superiors that he and his team were on the right track with this project. First, they needed to find a subject who could carry out a series of steps to bring the team back conclusive evidence of what really happened on that fateful morning in Dallas on November 22, 1963.

Mr. J had a person in mind that he felt could pull this project off. The team was now able to send a subject back with his memories intact of the future briefing. The subject was instructed to buy a camera with a telephoto lens. Next, he was to go to Dallas and set up his camera at a prearranged site. He was given explicit instructions to blend into the background and not get involved with the action. His job was to take pictures to prove where the shots came from that killed President Kennedy. After that, he was to take the film to the aforementioned bus locker and lock it up. Mr. J's team had already taken the trouble of going to Dallas and making a duplicate key for this specific locker. Once the subject had locked the film up, he was to submit an ad to be printed the next day in the local daily newspaper's lost-and-found section. This was a prearranged signal to inform Mr. J and his team of the status of the mission. The signal placed in the ad was "Little Nellie's dog was found." A team member of Mr. J's was stationed in Dallas in February 1964 and was to search for the classified ad on a daily basis. Once he saw the ad, he was to go to the bus locker and collect the film.

The film was processed. At the same time, the process in the chamber was reversed so that the subject's "mind print" was returned to the future. After Mr. J had the film developed in secret, he and his team analyzed the results. From Mr. J's description of the images caught on film by the agent, there was conclusive evidence that there was more than one person involved in the shooting and not a lone gunman as purported by the Warren Commission. More importantly, the mission was a success and went according to the detailed plan that Mr. J's team had written. The subject was debriefed and gave a very detailed account of his actions in the past. It was later found out that the target retained memory of his visit into the future.

After analyzing the results of the film, Mr. J contacted his superiors in Washington and set up an appointment to present his findings. He had 35 mm slides and blowups printed from the negatives which showed the most convincing evidence in support of Mr. J's hypothesis of multiple gunmen. At the meeting in Washington, Mr. J passed out a mimeographed copy of his report which included copies of the agent's photographs that supported his position.

When Mr. J finished his presentation and asked for questions, no one raised their hand. He told me that although the meeting went well, he felt his superiors were not interested in what he had to say. Mr. J's feeling was that they already knew what he was presenting and were listening just to be polite. Instead, he was asked to hand in all the negatives of the film. This was no surprise to him because this was S.O.P. (Standard Operating Procedure) for a highly sensitive Black Project. No records were to be kept. He was prepared for this and brought all of the negatives to the meeting. When he complied with their request, he was politely directed to wait out in the hallway.

Sitting in the hallway for over an hour and a half, Mr. J said that he felt like a prospective candidate for a job interview. Finally, he was called back into the committee room. The spokesman for the committee commended Mr. J on his enthusiasm for matters of National Security and personally thanked him for coming to Washington to deliver the presentation. The spokesman then announced that because of his presentation, the funding of Mr. J's team would be continued, but because of National Security concerns, he and his team had to sign security agreements and be deposed. This again was S.O.P. and was no surprise to anyone.

The speaker next commended Mr. J and his team on their professionalism and stated that they would all be compensated for their sacrifices. The speaker again thanked Mr. J and announced that the interview was at an end as he wished him a safe return to BNL. Before Mr. J could leave the room, the speaker also reassured him that he and his team would have their contract extended for another twenty years.

During the course of my discussions with Mr. J, I asked him why the subject did not interfere and stop the assassination. Mr. J replied that directions supplied by the EBE included a warning not to tamper with events in the time stream. They were directed only to observe for a complete historical record of the event. If they were to interfere with the time stream, insurmountable damage would occur. Mr. J said that time paradoxes causing rippling effects could even endanger this planet. I did not know what a paradox was or what he was alluding to but made a mental note to look up the term and frame a question later.

As Mr. J told me about these events, we were standing in the lab and this made an impression on me. It would not have been so real had he told me about the events in a park. I have to admit that I was very excited at the prospect of traveling in time. Before we left the subject of the Kennedy assassination, I had to ask him a question that was gnawing at my brain. The general public was informed that it was a "lone gunman," but Mr. J had stated that there was more than one shooter. When I asked Mr. J who the other shooters were, he answered that that was not the point of the exercise. It was to prove the capabilities of his team. When he brought the subject of the assassination up at his meeting in Washington, he had the feeling that his superiors knew the answer and did not want him to broach the subject. But, before he left the room, he felt that he had to learn the answer to that question. So, he pulled one of the committee members off to the side and asked him "off the record," who was responsible for the assassination. Mr. J was warned that this information was extremely dangerous, and if he knew, he should be prepared for the consequences. Mr. J said that he understood this but still wanted a definitive answer. He was told that it was a united effort by the Cubans and factions of organized crime who were responsible for killing the president, and if the general public knew this, there would be a general revolt and our way of life would be in danger. This was the answer Mr. J was given and later related to me.

After being told the above and other related information regarding what was really going on at Brookhaven, this assassination stuff did not phase me one bit. I knew by then that there were some really strange things going on there, so I kept my promise and did not say anything about it until now.

As far as time travel research, Mr. J said that there was a great temptation to send people from their older to their younger selves to "correct the wrongs" of the past. But, after considerable thought about the consequences of tampering with the time steam, he said that they had to be very careful where his team went next. He ended by saying that this is why they never sent anyone back to kill Hitler. This action might have caused irreparable damage to the time stream. He added that it was a good thing they did not because the EBE's were monitoring their progress; and because of his show of good judgment, the EBE's were about to volunteer additional information.

CHAPTER TWENTY-THREE

23

ANNUAL REPORT

While Mr. J and I were still in the first sublevel of the secret lab, he stopped his reminiscence of the early events at BNL and stated that because of his experiences, he knew for certain that everything happens in life for a reason and that it was all part of a master plan. He did not relate whose master plan it was.

Mr. J went on to say that the EBE's told him this and that mankind had been under observation and their guidance for a long time. Up until now, the EBE's thought that we were too primitive and violent a society which was not mature enough to handle the gifts that they could bestow upon mankind. Mr. J said that all this began to change when he and his team did not exploit the chamber for personal gain. This was the test that the EBE's had designed, and they rewarded him and his team with additional information to supplement what they had sent already. He revealed that the EBE's were waiting for us to mature to the point that we could accept what we would be told.

Relating that the EBE's had sent emissaries to the Nazi regime, Mr. J said they felt that their society was too corrupt and would eventually fall.

Mr. J next stressed that it was a great responsibility and honor bestowed upon us that the EBE's had changed their minds and were willing to help us and not hinder our progress as they had in the past. Stopping Mr. J's speech, I asked him what exactly he had meant by that? He continued to say that because of our history of violence towards one another and lesser species, the EBE's had taken steps to retard our progress. Asking him to elaborate on this, he stated that this was not the time and place for a history lesson. Suffice it to say that Mr. J hinted that the EBE's made appearances in order to scare and frighten the inhabitants of Earth in such a way that they would stop their war making. He stated that they did this by flying over the battlefields and discharging their energy weapons harmlessly into the sky or the ground. In some cases, they even controlled the weather so as to hinder battles. And, if this strategy did not work, the EBE's would resort to kidnapping the leaders in full view of both opposing forces. This drastic measure could end a conflict. He ended by saying that this is how the EBE's made an appearance in our history books as gods riding fiery chariots and thus into our mythology.

Stating that I was not here to learn about the origins of the gods, Mr. J said I needed to see how our society had evolved enough to learn the true nature of the fascinating universe that we live in. He went on to add that the EBE's intention was not to frighten mankind but to show them the road to enlightenment and said that this is how a remote tribe in Africa had learned about the location of the star Sirius-B. It was not until the invention of the radio telescope in the 1950's that astronomers learned of its existence and they were shocked to find out that a "primitive" tribe in Africa, without the use of a telescope, knew of the location of a very distant star.

I asked Mr. J what gifts the EBE's have to offer man, but he did not want to elaborate. He told me that the EBE's wanted us to find out our own answers. They thought that we would grow more as a people if we had to work for the answers as opposed to having them handed to us. He said that the EBE's hinted that the answer to all of our problems, including disease, are right in front of us. All we have to do is abandon our preconceived notions and open our minds in order to solve our problems.

Mr. J then reiterated that the purpose of this trip was to show me the equipment and give me a brief history of its use. He said that this was a tremendous weight for him and his team to bear. But, in their long association, he felt secure in his team's ability to overcome any technical obstacles put in their path. He also added that he wanted me to know more about MAJESTIC-12 and the projects they were working on. At that point, he walked over to a nearby desk, removed a folder, and handed it to me. He told me to read it and then ask him some questions. He apologized that I could not take it home to study because it was "EYES ONLY" and there were no copies of this document. He added that he had "to pull a few strings" to even get this copy and could not risk their discovery. Mr. J said that this folder contained the MAJESTIC-12 "first annual report." It was a review of the President's special panel to investigate captured UFO's. He wanted me to see just how much time and energy the Government really expended in the research and exploitation of alien artifacts. I hastily scanned the report and silently handed it back to Mr. J. I really did not understand it at all. All I really needed to know was that the Government knew for certain that UFO's really existed and that they covered up their existence all in the name of National Security. After years of research, I finally found a copy of that report.

Please refer to Appendix A for the "MAJESTIC TWELVE PROJECT: 1st Annual Report."

Mr. J said that there was one more thing to add before we left the lab. At the time of the crash at Roswell, he told me that the Government researched the possibility of life in the universe and asked Robert J. Oppenheimer and Albert Einstein to write a paper on the possibility of EBE's and the possibility of a relationship with these inhabitants of celestial bodies and the government of the United States. He stated that both Oppenheimer and Einstein were told that this was a "hypothetical" proposition and an intellectual exercise. These two esteemed scientists had no idea of its real use. By 1947, the Department of Defense was collecting vast amounts of credible reports of sightings of UFO's. It was also exploring the possibility of what to do when they found one intact which by then had actually happened. MAJESTIC-12 had covertly asked these two scientists to write a paper on the remote possibility of this occurring. Mr. J said that he personally knew both of these gentleman and that Oppenheimer was on the ball and caught on to what was really happening. Einstein was just interested in the intellectual exercise and did not want to hear of any talk that it might be for real. He was not concerned in the least bit about this. Einstein just wanted to retire and work in his lab at Princeton. Mr. J continued by saying that this was a very insightful paper and that Einstein only read the rough draft. It was Oppenheimer who fleshed out the idea.

Mr. J said that after representatives of MAJESTIC-12 read this paper, they came to the conclusion that Oppenheimer was a communist at heart and could not be trusted with further knowledge of their work and even suggested that he be slowly removed from any further atomic weapons development. He told me that MAJESTIC-12 did not want to hear any communist rhetoric because they were deep within the fight against the Russians to suppress any knowledge of the EBE's existence.

Mr. J chuckled, "Sure, Oppie liked to bed communist women and was a socialist, but in no way was he 'in bed with them.' And these poor dumb bastards didn't know the difference. I think they were secretly jealous of the women he got."

Saying that this was enough for today, he said that we would not be back here until the Congressmen left and the lab went back to normal. We both went back upstairs, got into his car and drove home.

After years of researching Robert J. Oppenheimer, I agree with Mr. J's assessment of the esteemed physicist. He was a brilliant administrator chosen by General Grove and was the right man to handle the immense logistical nightmare called the Manhattan Project. But, when the project succeeded and a bomb exploded over Japan, the Government felt that they did not have to put up with his "life style" choices any longer. Once they had what they wanted, they cut him loose. Dr. Oppenheimer was a brilliant and original thinker but, like all great men, had quirks. He was human just like the rest of us. Even though he was very brilliant, he made some decisions that he had to pay for down the road. I eventually found a copy of the paper that Mr. J spoke of and quite agree that it was indeed very insightful and, I might add, thought provoking. By studying it and reading it "between-the-lines," I could also see the Government's point of view. The paper was a thinly veiled expression of the benefits of socialism. I would have thought that a person of Dr. Oppenheimer's intellect would have seen this for himself and hidden his real intentions. The paper was a little too transparent and that is where Dr. Oppenheimer ran into difficulty. As I said before, all of us are human and are not perfect. Dr. Oppenheimer was no exception to this rule. He made mistakes. More importantly, in the world of politics, he made enemies. When his project was scrapped and Japan surrendered, he was removed "from the loop." He was declared a security risk and his security clearance was taken away.

Please refer to Appendix B to see "Relationships with Inhabitants of Celestial Bodies" by Dr. Robert J. Oppenheimer and Albert Einstein.

24

IMMUNITY

Although the shock of the MJ-12 information was considerable, my young mind was more preoccupied with the thought that the President of the United States was killed by more than one shooter. I asked myself why this had to happen. What caused it and why couldn't it have worked out differently? In today's overly violent world, people have become indifferent to violence. Then, the world was a different place. There was "the summer of love" and absolute horror over the war in Vietnam.

On the way back home, Mr. J had tried to talk to me as a person and not a coworker. He said that he realized that he had told me something very difficult to understand, and he reemphasized that there was a purpose to all the madness. The purpose was that adversity causes personal growth. I had no idea what he meant by that but listened anyway. The soothing way he said it did a lot to calm me. He asked me questions about school and what my favorite subjects were. The way that he asked me made me feel that he was really interested in my life. It is funny, but at that age kids are not taken seriously, and here was an adult with an awful lot of responsibility caring about how I felt. It was just something I was not used to and I did not know how to react. Part of me wanted to cry for our dead president and the other part of me wanted to listen to Mr. J and keep a "stiff upper lip." So, Mr. J tried his best to relate to me even though he did not have kids of his own.

When he stopped the car at the front of my house, Mr. J said that I was doing fine and that I would be able to handle the next phase of my education. He said that in this phase, I had to trust his judgment and even though I might be frightened by what I saw, I was to have trust in him and this would see me through.

"Fine!" I said.

After Mr. J drove away, I stood there wondering what he was talking about. My thoughts did not last long because I heard my mother call, and I ran into the house.

The next day, when I came home from school, my mother informed me that I had a doctor's appointment. We drove down Carleton Avenue in Central Islip to the office of a doctor I will refer to as Dr. Smith. Even after thirty-two years, his family prefers that I not use his real name. All I can say about Dr. Smith is that in 1968 he was in his 70's and a well loved General Practitioner. He was so loved that, three years later, a school would be renamed after him, even when he was still alive.

My mother had told me that because of the upcoming flu season I had to have an inoculation. In those days, doctors were still using the reusable glass syringe. Just the sight of it would scare any kid to death and I was no exception. I did not like shots so my mother bribed me into getting a shot. She said that if I was brave, we would stop for ice cream on the way home. To the best of my recollection, I had never had a flu shot before so I did not think it was peculiar that I was getting one now. In fact, it did not even occur to me that it was strange that my sisters did not have to get one while I had to. My mother had explained to me that because they were "girls," they did not require an inoculation. I was eight years old and did know really know any better. I loved and trusted my mother and did what she said. When Dr. Smith gave me the shot and was all finished, he patted me on the head and handed me a glass jar that contained lollipops and said I could pick the one I wanted. He then told me to leave the room and said that there were a few things that he had to talk to my mother about.

Going to the waiting room, I picked up a copy of *Reader's Digest* and started to read the jokes. I really do not know how long I sat there, but I knew it was a long time. When we finally left the Dr. Smith's office, my mother stopped at the Big Apple supermarket for a few things she had forgotten. This had never happened before. Usually, my mother was very organized whenever she was in the grocery store. She never forgot anything. We were not long at the market before we finally made it to the ice cream parlor. On the way home, my mother announced that I would not be going to school for the rest of the week and that it was doctor's orders. She said that Dr. Smith said that I needed bed rest so my body could adjust to the shot. I did not feel sick in the least bit, but this news sure did make me very happy. It was a boy's dream: to stay home and not be sick.

As it turned out, I was in for the surprise of my life. I got very sick for almost two weeks. To tell you the truth, I had never felt so sick before. My mother was prepared for this though and bought a supply of chicken soup and fruit juice. I thought she was very smart, but from what I learned later, this is what the doctor had ordered. My mother said this was a typical reaction to the shot. My skin felt like it was on fire, and most of my time was spent going back and forth to the bathroom.

While I was at home, Mr. J paid me a visit. Concerned about my health, he said that he was sorry to see me in such misery and told me that it would pass and that I was given the shot to strengthen my immune system. I did not know what an "immune system" was and asked him to tell me about it. He stressed that biochemistry was not his field but explained that it is a system through which the human body fights against disease. Mr. J then asked me if I knew what "white corpuscles" were, and I told him that I did not. Next, he asked me if I knew what "white cells" were, and I answered that I did. He said that they were the same thing and were the "white knights" of the body. They were the first line in defense against attack. Mr. J then told me that getting the shot from the doctor was his idea because I needed one. When I asked him why I needed the shot, he said that all of his team had to get them periodically in order to boost the body's protection against disease. Everyone had to have protection against disease because it was "better to be safe than sorry." I went along with Mr. J's explanation even though I did not understand it. Mr. J was my friend and I trusted and respected his judgment. If he thought that I needed a shot, then I got one with no questions asked. Mr. J ended by saying that in about a week, when I felt up to it, we would go back to BNL. He did not speak of what he wanted to show me and just sat there and remained silent. Saying "good-bye" to me, he left the room. About a half hour later, I noticed Mr. J's car pull out of the driveway. When I asked my mother why he stayed around, she simply said that she had some family business to talk to him about.

25

ENCOUNTER

One week later, I began to feel better and my mother said it was time to get "lazy bones" out of bed and go to school. Actually, I did not really miss much school because my mother saw to it that I kept up with my homework. That same night, Mr. J came to dinner. He said that the reason he came by was to check and see how I was progressing. I told him that I felt a lot better and thanked him for thinking of me. Mr. J then said that he had gotten that sick when he had to get that shot. After he said that, I felt a lot better knowing that he had gone through the same thing as I had. We spent the whole time talking about football. Before he left, he pulled me aside and said that the following Saturday we would take an exploration into the unknown or, to quote the words of my favorite TV show, "To boldly go were no man has gone before." This last little surprise made me quite curious but, because of my past experiences at BNL with Mr. J, I thought I was prepared for anything he might "throw at me."

Before I knew it, Saturday arrived and Mr. J had come to pick me up to go to BNL. On the way, I could see that Mr. J was in a great mood, and all he could say was that he was glad that the "big shots" had come and gone.

In his own words, he expressed that he "was sick and tired of all the glad handing he had to do to keep the big shots happy." He said that the "big shots" came to have their pictures taken for "Atoms for Peace" and stated that the name itself was an oxymoron and chuckled. I did not have the least bit of a clue what he meant by that but decided not to ask him what he meant.

We arrived at BNL and went though the usual check points. Getting into the elevator this time, I was not in the least bit scared to get inside. By now, I knew it was safe even though I could see the floors go by as we went down. In the elevator car, there was a slot on the control panel for the insertion of an operating key. Mr. J inserted his oversized key into the slot and said that there was no button where we were going and that he had to use the "manual-override." Beside the slot was a handle he used for the manual-override. He said that where we were going was not to be advertised. After Mr. J said this, I was completely baffled. We started going deeper and deeper down into the subbasements. I really do not know what floor we went to because I stopped counting after ten. In other words, we went down well below 120 feet.

On the way down, Mr. J emphasized that if the President of the United States himself paid BNL a visit, he would not see what I was about to see. He said that less than a handful of people outside of his team knew of its existence. This was the best place to hide the country's most TOP SECRET project: in the center of a busy population. Mr. J explained that the reason these floors were excavated out of solid bedrock was because the "big shots" during the war were afraid of a Nazi attack and that these floors were constructed for the country to conduct secret research. Even to this day, BNL will not admit to the existence of these floors. Believe me, they are there.

When the elevator finally stopped at the very bottom, my ears popped, and Mr. J said that it happened because of the pressure difference. He told me to keep swallowing until the pressure equalized and that it would happen on the way up, too. Mr. J took a white rectangular badge out of his jacket pocket and handed it to me with the instructions to pin it on my shirt. He told me to let him know if it changed color.

The white rectangular badge Mr. J handed to me had a safety pin on the back to attach to my shirt. I had no idea what it was for and thought that it might be an ID badge. Today, this badge is called a "Rad Badge" and is used anywhere there is a chance of a radiation leak. It is a good thing Mr. J had not told me first because if he did, there was "no way in hell" I would have even set foot in the elevator. Back then, I did not know what radiation was. Today, I know what even a mild dose a gamma rays could do to me.

Before we left the elevator, Mr. J told me that this was the culmination of the work started upstairs and that it was located in the deepest part of the lab because of security concerns. What he did not tell me then was that the effects of their testing caused interference with television and radio reception. He also sidestepped the entire issue of radiation leakage. I believe he did this to avoid upsetting me any further and, deep down inside, he felt that it was safe because he was doing it himself.

After Mr. J died, I learned that his body had been severely ravaged by cancer. Could this be because he was exposed to various energy fields while working at BNL? I am not a physician and do not feel that I am qualified to make that judgment. All I know is that in the early years of atomic research, no one knew the dire consequences one could face ten to twenty years after being exposed to that type of radiation hazard.

When we stepped out of the elevator, I gasped. To say that the room was cavernous was an understatement. The only point of reference I can give is that the room was (to me, at that age) bigger than New York's Grand Central Station. As a child, it was a very impressive sight. What Mr. J had told me later was that this cavern was a natural formation created during the ice age by an underground river. He emphasized that he was not a geologist and said that very little blasting was needed to carve out the cavern. It was quite unlike the excavation needed to carve out the inside of Cheyenne Mountain for the Strategic Air Command (S.A.C.). Mother nature had done that for them, but the interesting thing was that, before they started construction or even thought of it, their "friends" had told them that it was there.

Even on a Saturday, there were men working down here. Mr. J had instructed me to keep silent. He went up to the "Operations Desk" to check in. I recognized the man at the desk from one of the card games and he greeted me. Mr. J was all business, took me by the hand, and led me down the very long hallway. On the way down the hallway, I noticed men working on a dull aluminum object. Mr. J instructed me to "pay no mind" to the men working and gave me the admonition that "all will be revealed." I distinctly remember this quote because it was often used in murder mysteries I liked to watch on TV. We went into a well-lighted room which reminded me of a doctor's office. Mr. J said that this is where the "chosen few" would be taken to wait until the experiment was ready. He directed me to have a seat as he sat in the chair next to mine. Mr. J then explained that the reason I had to have the shot was because our bodies did not have a defense against the bacteria I would be exposed to down here. He said that recent research indicated that the shot was not really necessary anymore, but he felt that I should have one anyway. I told him that I thought he was taking a big chance showing me this cavern. How would they guarantee that I would not talk? Mr. J hinted that this was already foreseen and taken care of.

What I did not know then was that Dr. Stevens and I had been taken into a lab at BNL and our memories had been erased and we were given the direction not to talk.

I did not stop and talk about my concerns to Mr. J because I trusted him, and I assumed that he trusted me. Mr. J next said that everything else he had shown me or talked to me about was just the "tip of the iceberg" and that it was all in preparation for this event.

I stopped him and asked him how they could pay for all of this. He said that was easy. After the war, there was an awful lot of extra money floating around and a lot of it was spent building this facility.

He chuckled and said, "Not even the bean counters at the G.A.O. (General Accounting Office) had the slightest idea of how much we spent or for that matter what was even here in the first place."

Mr. J said that all this was possible after we had passed the test given by our "friends." These "friends" had selected this place in order for us to learn more about them and "The Galactic Federation." He said that "privacy" was their number one concern and that is why this place was built.

I stopped him again, telling him that I thought that it was because of the war that this place was built. Mr. J answered by saying that it was just the first three subbasements that were built for the war. This one was built to suit the needs of their "new friends." He said that even though they were comfortable breathing our air, they needed a place that was safe from the outside. He hinted that even though the Federation was stable, the "friends" still had enemies. Mr. J said that this was not the place to discuss this further. He just wanted to set up the premise for the things he would show me next.

I then asked him if we could talk about the "thing" the men were working on in the cavern. He answered that he was getting to that and I was putting "the cart before the horse." Mr. J said it was a "conveyance device" and had a similar propulsion system to that of the "Type A" craft found at Roswell. He said that it used a "gravity drive" and that he would not say anymore because I would not understand him and get lost in the concept. Mr. J said that it basically used the force of gravity against itself. Instead of being pushed down by gravity as we are, the ship is pushed up or can hover by manipulation of gravity itself and achieve tremendous acrobatic feats. Saying that was all he could offer on the subject for now, Mr. J added that I would learn more later.

Having personally felt the "G" force exerted in a roller coaster at Coney Island, I asked him how the pilot was protected against the effect. Mr. J smiled and said that is why I was asked here in the first place. It was because of my brains. He added that not everyone would think of that and that is why it is overlooked in movies and TV. Although he said that he would not be too technical in his explanation, he told me in his own words that their "friends" showed them a solution that was exactly what Isaac Newton predicted when he said, "For every action there is an equal and opposite reaction."

When he tried to conclude the discussion by saying that their "friends" had shown them a pressure suit was no longer needed, I asked him what a pressure suit was and he explained that it was like the "space suit" the astronauts wear that inflates to hold the built up pressure to prevent the pilot from blacking out when he encounters significant "G" force. The pressure suit prevents the pilot's blood from pooling in his legs and forces it to remain in his head so he does not "black out." Mr. J continued by saying that the reason why the pilot of the "Type A" craft is not turned to hamburger is because there are sensors in the skin of the craft that tell an inside computer how much force to exert to counter the force outside the craft. I stopped and said that sounded very familiar to me. I told him that there was a device on the starship *U.S.S Enterprise* that was called "inertial dampeners" that did the same thing.

Mr. J chuckled and said, "The boys at the lab had a good laugh about that one. Gene Roddenberry doesn't know just how right he got it."

What Mr. J was talking about is the device that is constantly breaking down in the heat of battle on the *U.S.S. Enterprise*: the inertial dampeners. The device is cleverly never explained and just talked about when it is "off line."

Mr. J emphasized that all the other "gizmos" used on that show were, in his words, "Just a boatload of crap."

He continued by saying that because of this advanced technology, all of the acrobatics were very possible and "quite" fun and added that, because of the composite material that the craft's skin is made from, there is no heat build up as the craft careens through the atmosphere. Mr. J said that he added that last comment to save me the trouble of asking him.

Next, I asked him what gravity really was. Mr. J answered that it was funny that I asked him that because in his words, "Eggheads all around the world are scratching their collective heads trying to figure out exactly what gravity is and here we are manipulating it 'easy as pie.'"

Mr. J then stated that the "Type A" craft referred to above is used only for "short hops" in planetary atmospheres and is not the primary mode of travel in the Galactic Federation. How the craft got here is a story in itself. He said that he would talk about that later.

Before we moved on to another subject, there were two things I needed to ask Mr. J. First, I asked him to repeat what he had said about a device in the craft that compensated for the inertia generated by the craft's movement. Mr. J answered by saying that their friends' technology was far beyond the scope of his understanding. Then, he said that a computer controlled the counter force to combat the inertia. This was the best description he could offer even though there was no way our computers could compute that fast.

Remember, this was in 1968 when computers were still in the "golden age" of using punch cards and big reels of magnetic tape. Mr. J went on to explain that the EBE's computers ran on light and not electrical current like ours did then. (Two years ago I.B.M. announced that they were developing a light based computer system.) When I asked Mr. J to explain exactly how it worked, he confessed that he did not fully understand it. He repeated that it was like a driver of an automobile who does not understand how to repair it when it is broken. He went on to say that there are generators placed in the space craft that supply gravity inside the cabin when it is in space and also counteracts the force of inertia by a feedback loop with sensors in the craft's outer skin. He reiterated that nobody on his team understands it and said that the EBE drones perform the maintenance for it.

My second question was about the outer skin of the craft and how it handled the heat generated by the friction of the atmosphere. Again, he said that he did not understand it and could only use terminology that he was experienced in; not what the EBE's called it. All he could say was that it was some type of polymer that does not get hot at all when it runs flat out in a planet's atmosphere. He ended by saying that the way U.S. space craft handle this is by having a heat shield burn up instead of the capsule. The material the outer skin was made of was harder than a diamond. When they tried to cut it, they could not even scratch it. The EBE's had designed it to be a type of armor that could counteract the impact of micrometeorites and not use a "force field" commonly used in the television series that I loved so much. Mr. J terminated this line of inquiry and said that there was still plenty more that he had to tell me.

As Mr. J was talking to me, a gentleman dressed in a blue jumpsuit entered the room. He had blonde hair and blue eyes and his face radiated warmth and understanding. He did not say anything, but I could hear him talk to me and not with my ears. I could hear him in my head.

The man went on to say that I should not be afraid and this was the primary way his people communicated to each other. I was so shocked by this development that I got up from my chair and headed for the door. Before I could run out of the room, I was stopped by Mr. J and the visitor. Mr. J told me to "calm down" and instructed the visitor to talk to me normally.

The visitor had a fair complexion and if he had not talked to me "in my head," I could easily have mistaken him for a Scandinavian. The man was about six feet tall and dressed in a light blue flight suit with a stiff collar. After I calmed down, Mr. J walked me back over to my chair. He next went and got me a drink of water and told me to sip it. While all this was happening, the visitor was silent and just looked at me with an angelic expression on his face. The man spoke up and introduced himself as John. He said he had another "formal" name but said that

I would have a difficult time pronouncing it. Asking him if he was from the Netherlands, he said no and that he was from someplace further away than that. When I asked him specifically where, he said that it was not important now. Mr. J then spoke up and told John that we were discussing the "Type A" craft and that I had some pretty interesting questions to ask him.

The man just sat there smiling, nodded his head in agreement, and said that everything would be all right now. I do not know what it was, perhaps the tone of his reassuring voice, but I believed him instantly. John asked me if I had any questions for him. I answered that I just wanted to know how he did that in my head. He smiled and said that I was capable of doing it, but I had not been taught how. He said that my society was based on aggression and that is why we have to shake hands when we first meet someone. It goes back to the era when men had to check for hidden weapons. In his world, people love and trust one another and there is no need to shake hands because of the more personal nature of their communication. In his world, they do not tell lies to each other because they cannot. This has made his world a very peaceful place. I asked him again where this was, and he calmly told me to keep patient. In time, I would know. Usually, if I was given this reply, I would get angry; but when John said this I was very calm. Mr. J interrupted and told John that I wanted to see the ship that the men were working on. John replied that it was all right and that he and his people had nothing to hide.

I really did not know just what all this was about, but I figured that if this guy said it was "all right" to see the ship, I wanted to get out of my chair and go have a look. John added that he would stay in the office and suggested that Mr. J give me a tour of the ship and then of the facility.

Mr. J and I left the office and headed towards the ship. The next thing that came out of Mr. J's mouth really astounded me. He said that John did not have to go with us because he would know what we were seeing, feeling, and thinking. He said he did not know if John could control what we were thinking but would not put it past him and commented that it was truly amazing what he could do. As we arrived at the ship, Mr. J suggested that I walk up to it and touch its outer skin. The craft looked like two pie pans glued to one another, and I could not see any rivets or seams. It was dull gray in color. When I touched it, it felt as smooth as if there was nothing there. Mr. J said that it was constructed of something they could not even describe because the metal that it was made from was unknown and not even listed in the "periodic table." At the time, I did not know what a "periodic table" was but I knew better than to ask too many questions.

The ship was about fifty feet in diameter. The first thing they discovered about it was that it was very light for its size. I then asked him why it was round. He replied that the reason for its round shape is that when the ship encounters the atmosphere at high speeds, the shape disperses the energy generated when air molecules collide with the hull. He added that he and his team thought that this was one of the reasons the hull stayed cool during high speed flights. The other reason was that the material that the hull was composed of was very hard and at the same time surprisingly very light. Mr. J said that labs around the country have been trying to figure it out but had been hitting a major stumbling block. The major reason they had not "cracked that nut" was because it was not until recently that the EBE's had provided a sample for them to study. They have had a ship like this one for a very long time but were not able to remove a piece for research purposes it because it was so damn hard that they were not able to cut off a piece in order to study it.

When I next asked Mr. J how a ship this size got to be so far underground, he answered that this was a story in itself and would take hours to explain how it came about.

It was not until recently that I have found out just how the feat was accomplished. When I asked Dr. Stevens, he explained to me that the ship was transported there or, in his words, "teleported" there.

Mr. J next asked me if I wanted to go inside. He said that if we did, it would not be what I was used to on TV. I was really very interested in going inside, but I felt that I would rather see the rest of the facility instead and asked Mr. J if it would be all right to see it later. He answered that it was okay. Mr. J took my hand, and we walked in the semidarkness towards the end of the underground complex. Right then, I asked him how they could power up all the equipment this far underground.

Mr. J chuckled and said that it was a good question. He answered that even though there was sufficient power generated above ground, the team had to remain secret and decided to utilize fuel cells to supply the electrical power needed to run the labs and their equipment. He said that the fuel cells were similar to the fuel cells used to power the "Apollo Service Module." A nuclear reactor would draw attention to their work.

In 1839, the British physicist William Robert Grove (1811-1896) devised an electric cell that made use of hydrogen and oxygen and produced electricity as they combined into water; however, using methane or coal dust along with oxygen would be close to ideal. This was the type of fuel cell utilized in the vast underground laboratories underneath BNL that was built from the instructions supplied by the EBE's. The Apollo Service Module, like the space shuttle, uses fuel cells to generate electricity which does not utilize coal dust or methane in the chemical reaction. The Government vehemently denies the existence of such a power system.

Nuclear reactors were deemed too dangerous and cumbersome for this purpose and were also outlawed by a treaty signed by the Soviet Union and the United States during the Sixties. Because of the danger of nuclear contamination and weight restrictions, NASA (the National Aeronautics and Space Administration) had decided to utilize fuel cells without the methane or coal dust additive to generate the needed power during spaceflight.

Mr. J next took me into another lab. It really did not look any different than one of the labs upstairs. Mr. J then said that this lab was for spectral analysis of material recovered at the Roswell crash. I really had no idea what spectral analysis was. Before I could ask him about it, he volunteered an explanation. He said that spectral analysis is like what astronomers use to analyze the chemical composition of stars. A sample is heated and the light that it gives off is shown through a prism and these spectral lines determine the composition of the sample. I knew what a prism was because I had one at home. This was a very intriguing process for me, and I could not wait to get home and go to the library so that I could learn more about it. Mr. J continued by saying that the material analyzed from the crash was very interesting. It was not that the materials used were new or undiscovered, but the intrigue was in the combination that they were used. The scientists researching the material had no idea that elements could be combined in such a fashion. All of them wanted to write papers about this and hoped to win a Nobel Prize. In fact, he said that an extra security lid had to be placed on the research to ensure that the publicity seeking scientists would not bolt and run off and publish. Mr. J added that these scientists were not his men but came from Los Alamos and were soon replaced.

Mr. J walked me over to a cabinet against the far wall and pulled out some samples of material. He stated that this was a sample of the cloth found on one of the dead EBE's from the craft. He next showed me enlargements of the photo micrographs of the material. This was a photograph of a microscope slide of the material. He told me to pay strict attention to the weave and said that when the material was analyzed, the scientists could not believe the combination of materials. In other words, it was a combination not in existence before the crash at Roswell. When they tested this material, it proved to be flame resistant and even bullet proof. Mr. J said that a piece of this material was now in the process of being funneled into the chemical industry by an agent working in the Pentagon. They hoped that some industrious chemical engineer would pick up on its potential and manufacture it as this material would be of great use to the police departments and the military in developing light weight bullet proof vests. Today, this material is known as Kevlar and has saved many a policeman's life in gun battles. Evidently, the flame resistant property of the fibers has never been fully realized. In one of my favorite TV shows, *The Untouchables,* I had seen bulletproof vests which were very large, heavy, and made from woven steel. I was truly fascinated by this lightweight composite material.

Suddenly, I looked up for a second at Mr. J and saw a strange expression on his face as he shook his head to say, "NO!" At the same time, I felt a gentle pressure on my right shoulder. As I turned slowly to my left and just before I fainted, I glimpsed a two-legged being staring intently at me through two beady reptilian eyes.

To be continued . . .

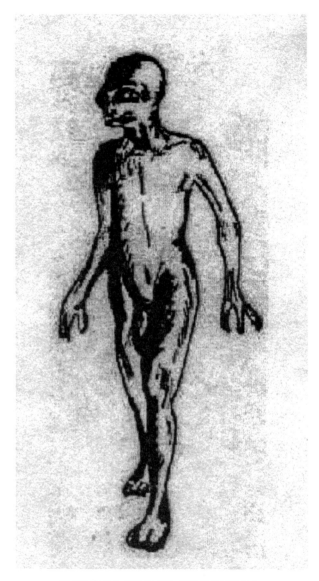

DINOSAUROID CREATURE

Above is a line drawing of the creature I saw in the underground at Brookhaven. I prefer to use the term "dinosauroid" to describe the alien.

EPILOGUE

The sudden and abrupt end to the story you have just read was disconcerting to me when I read it. I asked Wade if he could elaborate more on what he saw in the underground or if he could at least give us a summary. Unfortunately, he said that would not be possible. He said that in order to talk at all about the alien situation, it would require a lot more writing as the entire subject is so complex. In other words, that means another book. I informed him that this might not be feasible due to economic circumstances. What he did have to say was the following:

"Continued research has allowed me to uncover information crucial to an understanding of the impact of "advanced technologies" in past events. Insights continue to emerge as the technology, enormously complicated yet subtle, inspires new discoveries. The source of this technology, its impact on our society, and its eventual uses form the basis for my interest and passion. The fact that I was privy to such information at a tender age is astounding to me. Only recently have the events of my life slowed down to such an extent that I am able to meditate upon the importance of the revelations I still hold in my mind. It is as if one part of my brain was shut down and woke up the other. This has become the exciting part of life's journey that keeps me from utterly disparaging the future.

Consider the possibilities. An alien race actually exists. They have initiated contact many times with humans at least since the earliest moments of recorded history. There seems to be no distinction between the aliens who have contacted us in the 20th Century and those who contacted the ancient Egyptians, Mayans, and Aztecs. They have been making contact with humans for a long time, and yet we know so little about them. What was the nature of the contact? Was it all benign or were there times when humans or aliens lost perspective, patience, or nerve? How much of human history has already been affected by them? Today, we realize that for the last fifty-three years, aliens or an alien race has been attempting to affect human history by contacting the principals. We have substantial evidence for this, yet many in our government continue to insist that this is a bogus idea.

I am not really concerned with why the Government does not want to reveal the truth but only with what truths have yet to be revealed. Thus, I have offered the results of both of my regression therapy and my research. I have taken considerable pains to avoid discussing any recollection that cannot at this time be connected to fact. I have also omitted recollections which, for now, seem too farfetched even for me to seriously consider. In addition, I have provided United States Government documents of activities regarding the presence of EBE's to underscore some of what I have said (see Appendix C). In my narrative, I made every effort to avoid exaggeration and hyperbole. Additionally, I have purposely used an understated tone consistent with the level of seriousness with which I approach my work on this subject. It is my fervent hope and sincere intention to answer the unanswered, to challenge the naysayers and debunkers, to uncover the truth about Roswell, the Philadelphia Experiment, and the secret work that was and is still being carried out at Brookhaven National Laboratory for the truth is no longer "out there" but "in here," and you can discover it for yourself."

Wade has added more documentation to his testimony in Appendix C, but there is also a considerable new piece of evidence that has recently come upon the UFO data front. There is also an interesting story that accompanies it.

When the manuscript for this book was completed, I sent a copy to Ariel Phoenix, the artist who did the cover for this book. At the time she was to begin the art work for the cover, she suffered a major theft which set her back considerably in many areas of her life and nixed her plans to do the cover. Subsequently, another artist was contracted to do the cover. When he was about to begin the cover, he suddenly disappeared. No one could find him and his phone was mysteriously disconnected. He did not have money problems. I began to wonder if a conspiracy was afoot. I soon found out that the second artist had found a document on the internet that had been obtained through the Freedom of Information Act and demonstrates that the Government was involved with a crashed flying saucer at Roswell. It is written on official letterhead to J. Edgar Hoover from Guy Hottel of the Strategic Air Command in

Washington, D.C. See Appendix D. The artist in question had posted this particular document across the internet as broadly as possible. Soon after, he disappeared. The timing was suspicious. He did not inform his business partners or anyone else as to his whereabouts. I eventually found out that after he received a copy of the manuscript of this book on diskette, it disappeared. At about the same time, this artist was listening to Haitian voodoo tape recordings in conjunction with his job. He subsequently suffered a form of possession that appears to be connected to the Haitian energy, but it also seemed directed at stopping this book from getting published.

If there was no conspiracy with this second artist, it was discovered that there was definitely a conspiracy with regard to the original artist. After all the time that had passed with finding and losing a new artist, Ariel was ready to do the job. As soon as she accepted it, she received a most peculiar email that was designed to harass and intimidate her. It was from an autonomous email address and taunted her with information about her earlier life that no one else would likely know. She was addressed with her original maiden name and was told, amidst other things, to sever her connection with myself.

These anecdotal stories about the artists demonstrates a "fear pattern" that has surrounded stories of UFO's and aliens for decades. Fortunately, this fear was superceded to the point where the book that you are reading could be produced. This brings us to another point about UFOlogy. Just because uncovering such information can create fear does not mean that people have to succumb to it. If you refuse to agree with the "fear patterns," you will be empowered to overcome it. Nowhere has this been more evident to me than my association with a woman who works at BNL as an English language teacher to Brookhaven scientists who speak English as a second language. My association with her goes back to some bizarre coincidences I experienced when I set out to write *The Montauk Project: Experiments in Time* with Preston Nichols.

In 1991, Preston suggested that I should go to Montauk Point with a "sensitive" and see what he or she picked up. He said I should find someone that was not recommended by him or connected to him in any way so as not to prejudice the investigation. Soon after, an acquaintance referred me to a woman named Yonda Ashley. She was the first person I had contact with in my own investigations. Unfortunately, this contact was very short.

Although I did not know it at the time, Yonda had a boy friend who was originally supposed to write Preston's story. I knew him as an acquaintance but had no idea he even knew Yonda. Six months earlier, I had visited Preston with him and several others. After that meeting, he backed down on the writing project and wanted nothing to do with Preston Nichols or the Montauk Project. He told me that I could go ahead and do it. I thought it over for about six months before deciding to take the job on. It was at that point that I called Yonda. She was very friendly on the phone and told me that I would get more than I bargained for with this investigation. Her sensitivities also told me that the subject matter of the Montauk Project was very real.

As it turned out, the boy friend had huge blocks on the subject of the Montauk Project and insisted she not have anything to do with me. Occasionally, I ran into the both of them, but he always made it clear he wanted nothing to do with Montauk. Yonda did say, however, that this man always ran down to the book store as soon as a new Montauk book came out and read them ravenously.

Eight years later, I ran into Yonda once again, but that boy friend was now in her past. She was surprised that I had made it thus far and had survived as well as I had. To my surprise, she was ready to work with me. As a certified teacher in New York State, she explained that forces were in motion to make her an English language teacher to the foreign scientists at Brookhaven National Laboratory. We both thought this was very funny in regards to our past history. She was not passionate about getting the job, but she learned that they could not fill the post. No one really wanted it and those who had tried it in the past could not handle it. Those in the hiring position sought her out with some vigor. Finally, she was hired and given a full security pass with access to the Brookhaven campus. In view of the current book, I have asked her to relay her experiences with me and with Brookhaven.

"In 1991, I received a call from Peter Moon related to a book that he was writing. The subject was to be about Montauk and the experiments that had taken place there. He was looking for an intuitive to go out to Montauk and had been given my name by a mutual friend who felt I was right for the job. After several conversations, I decided it was not in the best interest of anyone for me to overtly participate in the venture. Peter and I had intermittent contact throughout the years. It was not until June 1999 that we bumped into each other again. One month after our reunion, I was given the assignment to teach English at Brookhaven Laboratory to the scientists and their families.

"BNL has received a great deal of negative press in regard to crimes against the environment and humanity. BNL has a global reputation of questionable standing. The concern over these issues by the community and certain individuals within the scientific field is well warranted. The misuse of power is being shaken by books such as this one that challenges the current ethics of Science. We are in an age where Science is becoming accountable for its past and present actions. Yet, this is only one aspect of the scientific field. I have been at the laboratory for over two years and what I have come to know and love are the scientists that open their hearts and speak the truth pertaining to the issues of ethics, mind control and the like. We are at a tipping point of conscious evolution of the scientific field. In one conversation I had with a physicist from the Orient, it has been his experience that fifty percent of the scientists are spiritual scientists. They have the same concerns we have about humanity and the conditions of Earth. These are the voices that are penetrating the darkness that has surrounded scientific research too long. What I desire to bring to light is the side of BNL that no one hears or reads about. It is the enlightened aspect of BNL: the people that work and live there.

"I have had the opportunity to get to intimately know many employees and family members during my employment. They have opened their hearts and expressed their thoughts and feelings. Being an outsider at first, it was a struggle to be accepted by most of the scientists and residents that came in to my class. I weathered the storm and the tide began to change. In the midst of the struggle, I began to see something that I had not expected. Little by little, the conversations moved in the direction of politics, philosophy, education, natural methods of healing, yoga, tai chi, UFO's, UFO's and the Brookhaven connection, interdimensional existence, experiencing chi, opening the third eye, dolphin energy, spiritual science and the evolution of global peace. What is in their hearts is in ours. The wall of fear began to crumble in front of my eyes and each class became an open forum of questions, thoughts, and insights from some of the most intelligent and spiritual individuals I have ever met. They became the voices of the everyday people of their respective country, moved out of the shadows and connected with their hearts.

"With each step I took in establishing open honest communication, the more they did the same. My respect and admiration for this unique group of individuals grew and has become an enriching and life altering experience.

"During one class, a young scientist from Eastern Europe asked me what I did outside of BNL. I spoke to him about my work in the arts where I use visual art as a vibrational tool to help others understand the interdimensional aspects of reality. I brought to the table the language of geometric patterns and how to understand this language of complex patterns that resonate frequencies that one reads with the third eye; thereby setting up the potential for an interdimensional experience. Each one in the class added to the topic from their chosen field of study. They brought evidence from their experiences to build upon and construct a model of the existence of other dimensions and how to consciously tap into them. They did not dispute or ridicule my research in the creative arts. They wanted to know more. They asked me to do a session and I did so the following week.

"The scientists listened to music, worked with aroma, chimes, and crystals to experience energetic fields. When they began to relax, they started to paint and draw. When they were finished, they shared their process with the group and what they thought and felt while they were drawing. They spoke of the symbolic representation of the drawings and related it to meditation and the dream state that they had explored. None of them had ever consciously felt energy and the scientist from Poland asked me to show him how to feel chi. He reached his hand out to me, and I to him. I told him that the more he experienced the life force and applied it to his work, the greater his effect would be on global enlightenment for humanity. He agreed. The bridge of science, creative arts, and spirituality was being explored and established with a small group of scientists at BNL.

Within the administrative framework of the laboratory, there are some that are challenging the comfort zones of established protocol for the management of the lab, scientific standards, and living conditions for the people. They envision Brookhaven as becoming a global model that will set the pace for other laboratories world-wide; thus uplifting science to a position that enhances humanity. There is a desire to connect with the public in an open and honest forum that will end the mystique surrounding Brookhaven. The process is slow, but they are persistent.

I envision Brookhaven Laboratory as a global, galactic, and universal crossroads. My experiences have restored my faith in science. I see the bridges being constructed by dedicated individuals who have the concerns for humanity and the Earth in their thoughts, actions and most importantly, in their hearts. We are living at a time where we will see the end of the old system and the rising of love based science. The process has already begun and cannot be stopped. There is hope!"

Yonda Ashley

Yonda is quite correct when she states that more and more scientists are turning towards spirituality. This has been a key subject in international physics conferences, too. There is reason to hope that more scientists will come forward and share their experiences.

Even more importantly, Yonda has openly stated that she is not afraid of any consequences from having her name appear in this book. She wants to set an example that people need not be afraid to come forward. Fear is only as strong as your mind allows it to be. If Yonda loses her job over this book, she is not afraid.

Of course, this does not mean an immediate end to "spook" projects, another name for black operations which seek to exploit or control individuals or the entire population. When Preston Nichols and I wrote *The Montauk Project: Experiments in Time* almost a decade ago, we threw out some threads of information in order to get more. It has proven a successful operating basis in the past, and I am hopeful that this book will encourage other citizens to come forward with what they know in order to dissolve the mystery and hostility that has surrounded Brookhaven National Laboratory.

Fear is only a state of mind.

Please send your information regarding abusive practices at Brookhaven to the following address:

Brookhaven Investigation
PO Box 769
Westbury, NY 11590

The work is not yet over.

Peter Moon
Long Island, New York
July 16, 2001

.

APPENDIX A

On the following pages is the first annual report of the Majestic-12 group entitled "MAJESTIC TWELVE PROJECT: 1st Annual Report." These are from photo copies of the originals. Use reading glasses if necessary so as not to strain your eyes. These documents can also be easily found on the internet where they have been translated into more readable English.

States Air Force
Rear Admiral Paul F. Lee, Chief, Office of Naval Research, United States
Navy
Admiral John Gingrich, Director, Security and Intelligence, AEC
Dr. J. Robert Oppenheimer, Chairman, General Advisory Committee, AEC
Jerome C. Hunsaker, MIT, National Academy of Sciences
Detlev W. Bronk, Chairman, National Research Council
Dr. Hugh L. Dryden, Director of Aeronautical Research, NACA
Dr. James H. Doolittle, Shell Oil

FOR
INCLUSION

TOP SECRET Central Intelligence Agency Information Report CIA/SI 28-55
entitled: A DIGEST OF WORLD WIDE UNIDENTIFIED FLYING OBJECT INTELLIGENCE
MATERIAL AS CONTAINED IN THE ARMED FORCES SECURITY AGENCY SIGNALS, RADAR,
COMMUNICATIONS, AND HUMAN INTELLIGENCE OPERATIONS IN THE FIRST FIVE YEARS

Note: This report has been coordinated with the Joint Intelligence
Committee, the Air Technical Intelligence Center,
and the Intelligence Advisory Committee

Approved for More
Date

A95(

WARNING: This document contains sensitive intelligence information
affecting the national defense of the United States, within
the meaning of Title 18, Sections 793 and 794, of the U.S.
Code, as amended. Its transmission or revelation of its
contents to or receipt by unauthorized person is prohibited.

MAJIC

MAJESTIC TWELVE PROJECT

Director
Dep. Director
Adm. Officer
Pres. & Control
Records & Pub.

Asst.
Visual
Statistical
Correspondence
Copies
Filed at....

1st Annual Report

A-1762.1-J1

A REVIEW OF THE PRESIDENT'S SPECIAL PANEL TO INVESTIGATE THE CAPTURE OF UNIDENTIFIED PLANFORM SPACE VEHICLES BY U.S. ARMED FORCES AND AGENCIES

PANEL

CHAIRMAN, Dr. Vannevar Bush, 4901 Hillbrook Lane (Phone, REpublic 6700, branch 5481)

General J. Lawton Collins, Deputy Chief of Staff, United States Army
Major General Luther D. Miller, Chief of Chaplains, United States Army
General Hoyt S. Vandenberg, Vice Chief of Staff, United States Air Force
Lt. General Lewis H. Brereton, Chairman, Military Liaison Cmt. AEC
Maj. General George C. McDonald, Director of Intelligence, United States Air Force
Brigadier General George F. Schulgen, Director, Plans and Policies, United States Air Force
Rear Admiral Paul F. Lee, Chief, Office of Naval Research, United States Navy

P. Problems in Relation to Biological Warfare Programs.

Q. Problems in Relation to Genetic and Pharmaceutical Development Programs.

N. Problems in Relation to New Materials Development.

I. Problems in Relation to Planned Future Rocket Development Programs.

J. Problems in Relation to Nuclear Propulsion Development Programs.

K. Problems in Relation to Intelligence Gathering and Analysis.

L. Problems in Relation to Foreign Policy and National Security.

M. Problems in Relation to Domestic and Constitutional Issues.

N. Problems in Relation to Social, Religious and Scientific Reaction.

O. Problems in Relation to the Cold War Development.

P. Problems in Relation to the Government Policy of Control and Denial.

FOR OFFICIAL USE ONLY

834021-72

RESTRICTED

"NOT FOR PUBLIC INSPECTION"

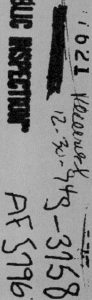

I. PURPOSE:

The aforementioned panel under the direct presidential direction signed on 26 September 1947, has been tasked with responsibility of proving beyond to a most troublesome and disturbing phenomenon, that of otherworld visitation and what it portends for the human family. It is in this vein that the panel has addressed the problem and in providing possible answers.

II. TABLE OF CONTENTS

A. Nature of the Investigation.

B. Panel's Contribution to the TOP SECRET MAJESTIC Research and Intelligence Program.

C. A Review of the Military Assessment with Selected Comments Drawn from Conclusions of the JIC and IAC Members.

D. Problems in Relation to Technology.

E. Problems in Relation to Nuclear Weapons Development.

F. Problems in Relation to Biological Warfare Programs.

G. Problems in Relation to Genetic and Pharmaceutical Development Programs.

H. Problems in Relation to New Materials Development.

181

classified defense projects. Conferences were held with national security officials and leaders of private industry. Approximately 1,200 memoranda and intelligence reports were considered. The report presents this situation against a global background my estimates, current and projected, in both the U.S., and allied countries, and recommendations deemed to be sound courses of action for formulating plans and policies in light of recent developments.

3. All efforts have been made to identify the country or private concern which could have the technical and financial resources necessary to produce such a long-range flight. So far, no country on this earth has the means and the security of its resources to produce such.

4. A consensus reached by members of the panel, that until positive proof that the Russians did not attempt a series of reconnaissance flights over our most secure installations—the sightings and recovered objects are interpalnetary in nature.

5. The occupants of these planform vehicles are, in most respects, human or human-like. Autopsies, so far indicate, that these beings share the same biological needs as humans.

-2-

RECEIVED

~~TOP SECRET~~

III. CONCLUSIONS

1. Current studies of other-world visitation are in three phases:

   a. Technology exploitation

   b. Interplanetary travel

   c. Cultural communication

2. On 19 September 1947, the IAC, JIOA, and the JIC, reviewed a Top Secret intelligence report titled REPORT TO THE PRESIDENT, 1947, PARS 1-V MAJIC EYES ONLY, DTG 00019094U7, the report mentions? "A camp Limbo with your directive . . . af 9 July 1947, the attached "REPORT ON FLYING SAUCERS" is respectfully submitted. In consonance with your instructions, advisors from State, Treasury, War and Navy Departments assisted me on a two month exploratory mission concerning the reality of other-world visitation. The principle investigators and storage areas were visited. Successful efforts were made to reach scientists of all levels as measured by their work in classified defense projects. Conferences were held with national security officials and leaders of private industry. Approximately 1,200 memoranda and intelligence reports were considered. The report presents this situation against a global background my estimates, current and projected, in both the U.S., and allied countries, and recommendations

2. In third(digest) primary attention has been paid to information of bio-medical intelligence interest, particularly in the BW program. Bio-medical intelligence is only one of the substantive fields covered by these Interrogation Reports.

3. For the most part, the sources interrogated were not trained observers, and their stories indicate they have been subject to the familiar pitfalls common to all eye witnesses. It must be emphasized that, because the interrogators used were not always specialists in this phenomena of celestial sciences, there is much lack of detail.

4. Because of the unique nature of the material under study, a multi-layered security structure has been in effect. Most of the results have been given to private research and development labs for further study.

5. MAJESTIC SHSP are currently focused on Psy-Op development for Cold War CI activities.

6. Utilisation of Paperclip specialists has yielded valuable results in new weapons research in areas of flight dynamics, biological and chemical agents, mind control, and intelligence gathering techniques.

-3-

IV. DISCUSSION

A. Nature of the Investigation.

An analysis has been made of the first one-hundred intelligence reports in the ATIC Interrogation Reports and the UIAFR EXPLOITATION-MAJESTIC SERIES 1-25, prepared by the Military Intelligence Section of CRC/IPU in order to establish what material of flying saucer intelligence value concerning the UIAFR is available in these reports.

1. The ATIC Interrogation Reports, numbered 1 to 93 (the last dated December, 1950), present significant information on a broad variety of subjects and areas where witnesses were detained subsequent to the post-1947 incident. The unpublished documents constitute records of interrogation derived from the accumulated reports on interviews of selected witnesses from New Mexico and military personnel involved in removal of evidence.

2. In this (digest) primary attention has been paid to information of bio-medical intelligence interest, particularly in the BW program. Bio-medical intelligence is only one of the substantive fields covered by these Interrogation Reports.

3. For the most part, the sources interrogated were not trained observers, and their stories indicate they have been subject to the familiar pitfalls common to all eye witnesses. It must be emphasized that, because the interrogators used were not always specialists in

2. For the clarification of published reports or for elaboration of the information of *fragmentary nature*, resort may be had to the ABC files of *unpublished data* as well as to the possibility of reinterrogating the sources.

C. Review of the Military Assessment

With current deployment obligations, troop commitments, and few air groups with stand-by fighters with radar capability, the Joint Chiefs are unable at the present time, to effect a complete and all-encompassing defense plan that would guarantee the protection and well-functioning of the national political order. Personnel, material, and logistical requirements for such a defense would deplete current resources. If such a crisis should occur—in government failure to defend and assure the public's trust, it is the belief of the Joint Chiefs, that the following would insure: insecurity and mistrust; employment of subversive agents; infiltration; incitement of disorder and chaos to disrupt normal economy and undermine popular support of government and its leaders; seizure of authority without reference to the will of the people.

D. Technology

It present, the ability to reconstruct the technology that may be *gone ahead* of us, the boost to our current efforts would be *incalculable*. Areas such as aircraft and missile design would benefit only after a working understanding has been achieved. Weapons sciences will follow.

-4-

B. Panel's Contribution to MAJESTIC

1. The contribution of the President's Special Panel to the MAJESTIC TWELVE PROJECT has supplemented information on the ULATW Program which could not be obtained in any other way. Although only a small part of the project, interrogation is technical and bio-medical field has produced at least 6,973 items for the files of Military Intelligence, ONC/IPU. Of these items, 3,764 have been published (up to December, 1950) in the ULATW EXPLOITATION-MAJESTIC SERIES. The coverage of the New Mexico incidents, from the over-all intelligence point of view, has been very good. (After the Panel's review was initiated, ONC/IPU published in March 1951, the summary "MAJESTIC SERIES," No. 98 and No. 99, of the series titled "New Medical Facilities for Biological Warfare; New Genetic and Pharmaceutical Development Programs." These summary reports have apparently made of much of the ABC file material since published "Medical Items" in the AEC file material since 6,014 items are now reported as published "Medical Items" in the "Interrogation Reports" — see MAJESTIC SERIES, No. 98, page 4.)

2. For the clarification of published reports or for elaboration of the information of fragmentary nature, resort may be had to the AEC files of unpublished data as well as to the possibility of reinterrogating the sources.

C. Review of the Military Assessment

With current deployment obligations, troop commitments, and few air groups with stand-by fighters with radar capability, the Joint Chiefs

• A Zika-virus not totally understood, but, give promise of the ultimate
BW vessels. The danger lies in the spread of airborne and bloodborne outbreaks
of diseases in large populations, with no medical cures available.

G. Cosmetic and Pharmaceutical Development Programs

Current research in U.S. and U.K., can be accelerated when studies
are complete. Understanding the human makeup through EBR research will bring
a varied wealth of information in how cells replicate themselves and may help
in developing new drugs and markets. Healthcare industries are considered the
best source of R&D for DoD programs.

H. New Materials Development

Conclusions reached by the Air Material Command in 1948, upon
the close examination of the material structure of the Corona and Oscura
Peak, N.M. sites, compelled the Air Force to launch a new machinability
research program. Samples tested and evaluated by the LMC, suggested that
future materials would have to incorporate new alloys and composites, if
space exploration and hypersonic dynamics are to be achieved. As a result,
new machining techniques are underway for high-temperature alloys and
titanium.

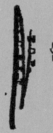

-5-

SECRET

E. Nuclear Weapons Development

Miniaturization of atomic bomb components is the goal of the AEC and the AFSWP. Studies at MIT indicate that such a technology is within reach before the decade is out. The apparent use of micro-circuitry found on the recovered platform indicates that miniaturization, low-power transmission, light conductor/sensitive components are required for interplanetary space travel. Atomic engines and nuclear propulsion technologies could be advanced based upon current use of hydrogen and electro-magnetic research and weapons components development in U.S. and U.K.

F. Biological Warfare Program

BW progress in U.S. and U.K., are in field test stages. Discovery of new virus and bacteria agents so lethal, that serums derived by genetic research, can launch medical science into unheard of fields of biology. The samples extracted from bodies found in New Mexico, have yielded new strains of a retro-virus not totally understood, but, give promise of the ultimate BW weapon. The danger lies in the spread of airborne and bloodborne outbreaks of diseases in large populations, with no medical cures available.

G. Genetic and Pharmaceutical Development Programs

Current research in U.S. and U.K., can be accelerated when studies are complete. Understanding the human makeup through DNA research will bring a varied wealth of information in how cells replicate themselves and may help in developing new drugs and markets. Healthcare industries are considered the [...]

on the engine being kept at HAFB. Integration of hydrogen base fuels
and electro-hydrodynamic technology, may open up for us development of
super-aerodynes with such S capabilities.

K. Intelligence Gathering and Analysis

Based on what is known of the technology and intelligence of the
visitors, it is fairly certain that there will be other sightings and
encounters of a spectacular nature. As to purpose and modus operandi,
we are not certain, but it is clear, that if these visitors had conquest
in mind, it would not be difficult for them, given their ability to
penetration our airspace at will, and their ability to jam radar, telephone, teletype transmissions, and teletype transmissions, let alone power grid.
So far, reports and sightings are blatant and deliberate, thus allowing
our intelligence agencies to gather good data. As to the analyses of
such reports, only a continuous view of sightings and encounters world-
wide, would provide enough data for a clear understanding of intent.

L. Foreign Policy and National Security

To date, only Great Britain, Canada, and the Soviet Union, are
contacted and appraised in the event invasion is eminent. It is the
current policy of the Administration that no other foreign countries
will be consulted or advised. The national security status of the
MAJESTIC operation exceeds that of the H-bomb development.

TOP
‗‗‗‗‗‗

-6-

I. Planned Future Rocket Development Program

There have been a number of failed high-altitude rocket launches to study radiation effects on living organisms. The Air Force's Project BLOSSOM, conducted at Holloman AFB, is but one example. V-2 rocket launches at the White Sands Proving Ground, N.M., have been knocked down by undetermined jamming. The source of the jamming is believed to come from UFO sightings on or near the range. Guidance systems are believed to be vulnerable and this presents a clear and present danger. Such keeper flights carrying nuclear weapons are too horrific to contemplate. Shielding of systems and circuits are underway.

J. Nuclear Propulsion Development Program

The AEC and NEPA are currently conducting research for advanced propulsion studies. Systems studies at Los Alamos, N.M., Oak Ridge, Tenn., and at Langley, Va., are attempting to duplicate the water drive and plastic core elements found on the engine being kept at HIFR. Interpretation of hydrogen base fuels and electro-hydro-dynamic technology, may open up for us development of super-aerodynes with mach 5 capabilities.

K. Intelligence Gathering and Analysis

Based on what is known of the technology and intelligence of the visitors, it is fairly certain that they will be other sightings and encounters of a spectacular nature. As to purpose and modus operandi we are not certain, but it is clear, that if these visitors had conquest in mind, it would not be difficult for them, given their ability to penetrate our airspace at will, and their ability to jam radar, tele-

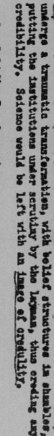

undergo a traumatic transformation, with belief structures in shambles, putting the institutions under scrutiny by the layman, thus eroding any credibility. Science would be left with an _image of credulity._

O. _Cold War Development_

This is one of the most dangerous phenomenon of the twentieth century. To _misidentify,_ a flight of space objects for actual Russian bombers, or to _dismiss_ Russian bombers as phantoms, is the most idiotic approach to take. Even though governments may distrust each other, it is the responsibility and creed of the military and intelligence professional to prevent wanton death and destruction of his country. It is advisable to _maintain some form of direct communication_ with a hostile enemy before taking false assumptions of his response _if false data wrongly indicates_ such. Even using the "Flying Saucer" ruse to create fear and confusion among your enemies leaders, could result in _accidental war._ Even our early analysis of the recovered _platforms_ in 1947, led to the wrong assumption that the Russians were preparing a sneak attack on the continent.

P. _Government Policy of Control and Denial_

One of the most difficult aspects of controlling the perception in the public's mind of government attempts of denial and ignorance—is _actual control of the press._ Until a clear intent is established with diplomatic relations firmly in hand, it is the recommendation of the President's Special Panel with concurrence from MAJESTIC TWELVE, that a policy of strict denial of the events surfacing from Roswell, N.M., and any other incident of such caliber, be enforced. I _inter-active program of controlled releases_ to the media, in such fashion to _discredit_ any civilian investigation, be instituted in accordance with the _provisions of the 1947 National Security Act._

-7-

N. Domestic and Constitutional Issues

In dealing with clear <u>violations of civil law and guarantees as
defined under the Constitution</u>, it has been discussed among members of
<u>MAJESTIC TWELVE</u>, that such protection of individual rights are out-weighed
by the nature of the threat. Only a declaration of war or a <u>national
emergency</u>, would give the government the power to enact <u>martial law</u> and
<u>recend individual rights</u>.

N. Social Religious and Scientific Reaction

It has been the downfall of great nations and cultures when a <u>new
reality</u> is not readily accepted by the <u>masses</u>. The social order was severely
ravaged by the last world war, with great damage to the religious dogma of
"earth without end," thus making a government disclosure irresponsible and
inherently dangerous. The scientific community would probably question
such a reaction as a world suffering from a Buck Rogers delerium and attack
anyone of their own ranks for believing such fantasy. Science itself, may
undergo a traumatic transformation, with belief structures in shambles,
putting the institutions under scrutiny by the layman, thus eroding any
credibility. Science would be left with an <u>image of credulity</u>.

O. Cold War Development

This is one of the most dangerous phenomenon of the twentieth
century. To misidentify a flight of space objects for actual Russian

193

...powered by a fusion reactor of sorts.

5. Lack of wiring, fuel system, cables, motors, hydraulics, intakes, exhaust, and surface controls, strongly suggests that the craft was designed to travel outside of our atmosphere.

6. The second craft that impacted at Site L-3, provided very little evidence that it too was similar in design, as the impact was vertical in nature and at very high speed. It is believed that the debris discovered on 2 July 1947, by local rancher was the result of a mid-air collision with an X-plane from MUR; another unidentified object; or possibly collided with both. Radar film and tower log do not explain the merging of three radar targets prior to collision and subsequent crashes.

7. There were five recovered bodies, two of which were found in a severely damaged escape cylinder, and the remaining three were found some distance away from the cylinder. All five appeared to have suffered from sudden decompression and heat suffication (recovery and autopsies of the occupants are covered in detail in a separate study ORAI SUIT within Projects 612 and 621 ULATI EXPLOITATION-MAJESTIC SERIES 4, P. 40-1027), as a result of damage sustained from unknown causes.—

-4-

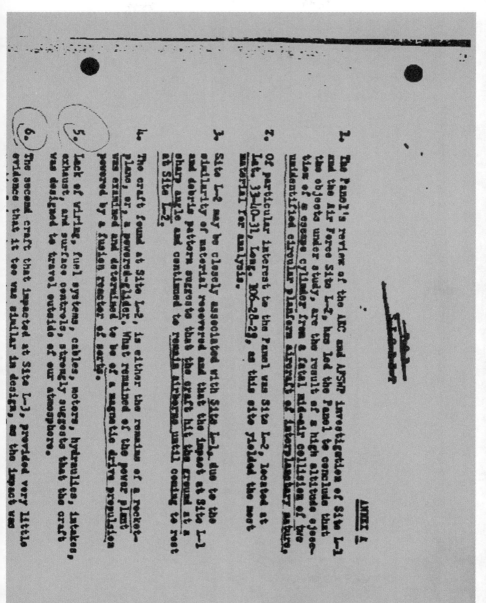

ANNEX A

1. The Panel's review of the AEC and AFSWP investigation of Site L-2 and the Air Force Site L-2, has led the Panel to conclude that the objects under study, are the result of a high altitude ejection of a escape cylinder from a fatal mid-air collision of two unidentified circular platform aircraft of interplanetary nature.

2. Of particular interest to the Panel was Site L-2, located at Lat. 33-40-31, Long. 106-28-29, as this site yielded the most material for analysis.

3. Site L-2 may be closely associated with Site L-1, due to the similarity of material recovered and that the impact at Site L-1 and debris pattern suggests that the craft hit the ground at a sharp angle and continued to remain airborne until coming to rest at Site L-2.

4. The craft found at Site L-2, is either the remains of a rocket-plane, or, a powered-glider, What remained of the power plant was examined and determined to be of a magnetic drive propulsion powered by a fusion reactor of sorts.

5. Lack of wiring, fuel systems, cables, motors, hydraulics, intakes, exhaust, and surface controls, strongly suggests that the craft was designed to travel outside of our atmosphere.

6. The second craft that impacted at Site L-3, provided very little evidence that it too was similar in design, so the impact was

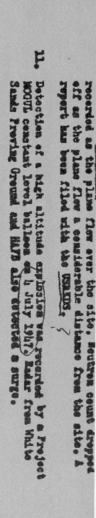

recorded as the plane flew over the site. Geiger count dropped off as the plane flew a considerable distance from the site. A report has been filed with the USAIDS.

11. Detection of a high altitude explosion was recorded by a Project MOGUL constant level balloon on 4 July 1947. Radar from White Sands Proving Ground and WWTB also detected a surge.

12. Parachute recovery team from WWTB were dispatched to Site L-2. Upon arrival, the team, realizing the nature of the crash, radioed instructions and marked crash site for the investigators that arrived later.

13. In the opinion of the senior AEC medical officer, current medical equipment and supplies are wholly inadequate in dealing with a large scale outbreak of the alien virus.

14. Facilities at Los Alamos and Wright Field are considered as lacking in the current climate.

15. On 26 September 1947, the first meeting of the MSC-1 was held to discuss the New Mexico incidents and how to implement the policy established by MJ-12 SSMP.

-3-

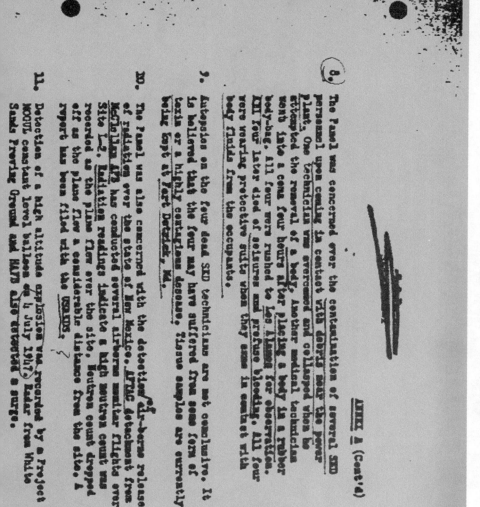

ANNEX A (Cont'd)

8.) The Panel was concerned over the contamination of several SED personnel upon coming in contact with debris near the power plant. One technician was overcome and collapsed when he attempted the removal of a body. Another medical technician went into a coma four hours after placing a body in a rubber body-bag. All four were rushed to Los Alamos for observation. XII four later died of seizures and profuse bleeding. All four were wearing protective suits when they came in contact with body fluids from the occupants.

9. Autopsies on the four dead SED technicians are not conclusive. It is believed that the four may have suffered from some form of toxin or a highly contagious disease. Tissue samples are currently being kept at Fort Detrick, Md.

10. The Panel was also concerned with the detection/air-borne release of radiation over the state of New Mexico. AFSWP detachment from McClellan AFB has conducted several airborne monitor flights over Site 1-2. Radiation readings indicate a high neutron count was recorded as the plane flew over the site. Neutron count dropped off as the plane flew a considerable distance from the site. A report has been filed with the USAEC.

11. Detection of a high altitude explosion was regarded by a Project MOGUL constant level balloon on 4 July 1947. Radar from White Sands Proving Ground and HATO also detected a surge.

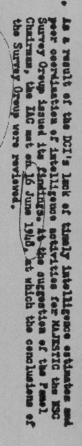

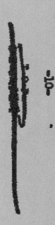

to the President, that a third party group from outside of the Government by established for the purpose of conducting a impartial and objective survey of the activities and personnel of the CIA.

5. As a result of the DCI's lack of timely intelligence estimates and poor coordination of intelligence activities for MAJESTIC the NSC Survey Group issued its findings. At the suggestion of the Panel Chairman, the IAC met on 16 June 1948, at which the conclusions of the Survey Group were reviewed.

6. On 18 February 1949, the IAC met for the purpose of proposing some changes to a CIA draft proposal on MAJCON activities.

7. General Joseph McCarney, with the assistance of Carlisle Knowledge and Robert Blum, prepare NSC 50/1 on 7 July 1949, the NSC adopted the recommendations of NSC 50/1 which directed the DCI to enlist the activities of the IAC in MAJESTIC intelligence activities.

8. MAJCON-1 meets with the President in May 1950.

9. Admiral Hillenkoetter leaves position as DCI on 7 October 1950.

10. MAJCON-1 with assistance of the Panel persuades the President to establish the Psychological Strategy Board on 4 April 1951.

-10-

TOP SECRET

ANNEX B

1. Upon the creation of the MAJESTIC TWELVE GROUP by special executive order dated 24 September 1947, and given power of authority by PDD/T-1, dated 26 September 1947, the Panel was empowered to assess and conduct a review of all available evidence and data collected by government and military intelligence agencies.

2. Because of the unique nature of the 1947/48 crisis, the Panel recommended to MAJCOM-1 that the authority-of-the-Secretary of Defense be invoked in order to implement NSCID No. 1/1.

3. A meeting was held on 8 December 1947 between CIA and IAC concerning the IAB, Dr. Vanevar Bush, Chairman of the Panel, requested the DCI to convey the contents of a letter from Dr. Bush to Secretary Forrestal, thus breaking the deadlock over issues concerning authority and policy making dealing with the New Mexico incidents and subsequent exploitation of the finds.

4. On 13 January 1948, the NSC, with input from the Panel recommended to the President that third party group from outside of the Government by established for the purpose of conducting a impartial and objective survey of the activities and personnel of the CIA.

5. As a result of the DCI's lack of timely intelligence estimates and poor coordination of intelligence activities for MAJESTIC the NSC Survey Group issued its findings. At the suggestion of the Panel Chairman, the IAC met on 16 June 1948. At which the conclusions of the Survey Group were reviewed.

summaries prepared by the Watch Committee. Beginning every Friday the President is briefed on world situation and on MAJESTIC via the CIA weekly Current Intelligence Review.

15. At the request of Panel member Cardinal Francis Spellman met with the President to discuss the containment within the Catholic Church and its hierchy of religious speculation if the 1947 sightings occur. Such containment was successful during the 1947 sightings when Cardinal Spellman met with the Secretary of War on 29 June. The President has been briefed on Defense Plan 47, which was written in part by the Panel member.

16. In support of the MAJESTIC program for developing atomic engines, Panel members and their association with the AEC, the Armed Forces and the National Advisory Committee for Aeronautics, have consulted MAJESTIC for the development of nuclear fission reactor for powered flight studies.

17. Atomic engines for aircraft built here on earth faces many difficulties because of size and weight of the reactor and radiation shielding. Such a nuclear power plant would give an aircraft unlimited range.

18. Panel members contributed to the writing of ULATI EXPLOITATION - MAJESTIC SERIES 5 title Hypersonic Small-Disturbance Theory, which gives consideration to a three-dimensional body fixed in a steady, uniform, hypersonic stream. The theory assumes that shock waves can be approximated by abrupt discontinuities and the planform body being thin, so that the slope of the local surface in the stream direction is uniformally small.

-11-

ANNEX B (Cont'd)

11. Panel member and MAJCOM-4 meet with MAJCOM-1 on 10 October 1950 along with members of IAC. The Chief of Global Survey Group desired estimates requested by the Pentagon concerning possible defense project for MAJESTIC LOGISTIC SSP-1.

12. On 6 December 1950, MAJCOM-4 alerts MAJCOM-1 of a breach in NEW Crewman of a UFO on a south-westerly course. HQ 12V alerted and dispatched a scientific team to El Indie-Guerrero on the Texas-Mexico border. MAJCOM-4 orders a recovery team from Project STORK and MCON DUS? to crash site. Team transport debris from crash site to HDQ HARP and to AEC laboratories at Sandia, New Mexico.

13. MAJCOM-1 enlists the Panel's eviction consultants for the purpose of advising the "Princeton Consultants."

14. On 28 December 1950, MAJCOM-1 is provided with the "Black Book" summaries prepared by the Watch Committee. Beginning every Friday the President is briefed on world situation and on MAJESTIC via the CIA weekly Current Intelligence Review.

15. At the request of Panel member Cardinal Francis Spellman met with the President to discuss the containment within the Catholic Church and its hierarchy of religious speculation if mass sightings occur. Such containment was successful during the 1947 sightings when Cardinal Spellman met with the Secretary of War on 24 June. The President has been briefed on Defense Plan 42, which was written in part by the Panel member.

16. In support of the MAJESTIC program for developing atomic engines, Panel members and their association with the AEC, the Armed Forces and the National Advisory Committee for Aeronautics, have consulted MAJESTIC for the development of nuclear fission reactor for several flight studies.

23. On 14 May 1948, MAJCOM-4 arranged for the promulgation of Air Force Regulation 20-30, which restored the powers of the SAB as agreed upon by Karman and LeMay in 1946.

24. MAJCOM-4 had a prepared speech read at a meeting of scientific advisors on 7 April 1949, highlighting new Air Force R&D organisation and structures on UFO research for ULATT. Karman enlisted the aid of a Panel member to persuade MAJCOM-4 to endorse a separate establishment free from AEC and Pentagon control.

25. On 6 January 1950, a plan was presented to the Air Staff Council for separate R&D for ULATT.

26. On 23 January 1950, Research and Development Command and the Air Staff Deputy Chief of Staff for Research and Development was created.

27. In May 1951, Panel member MAJCOM-4 endorsed Karman's creation of IDEW and his presentation at the Pentagon of a lecture called "Mobilisation of Scientific Effort in Western European Countries."

-22-

APPENDIX B (Cont'd)

19. MAJCOM-4, a member of the Panel was instrumental in supporting the the creation of the Air Force's Scientific Advisory Board which MAJCOM-5 endorsed.

20. MAJCOM-5 recommended to the Air Force Chief of Staff, that the Top Secret report Where We Stand, be the basis for USAF development. MAJCOM-5 urged the CoS to enact the ideas of another report Science, the Key to Air Supremacy. Major General Curtiss LeMay Staff Director of Research and Development seconded MAJCOM-5's views.

21. The Panel Chairman argued for funding for air defense projects that would be useful in combating the new menace instead of developing ballistic missiles, which have proved to be useless.

22. On June 15 1947 Dr. Theodore von Karman chaired the first meeting of the SAB and discussed how the Air Forces could prepare for a possible air attack in light of the numerous UFO sightings over the U.S.

23. On 14 May 1948 MAJCOM-4 arranged for the promulgation of Air Force Regulation 20-30, which restored the powers of the SAB as agreed upon by Karman and LeMay in 1946.

24. MAJCOM-4 had a prepared speech read at a meeting of scientific advisers on 7 April 1949 highlighting new Air Force R&D organisation and structures on UFO research for USAF. Karman enlisted the aid of a Panel member to persuade MAJCOM-4 to endorse a separate establishment free from AEC and Pentagon control.

Field Company signed sworn statements that they saw the One-
Fourth Norfolk Regiment disappear in a unusually thick brown
cloud which seemed to move and rose upward and vanished. There
were no traces of the regiment nor their equipment. No explanation can be found in the historical records of the Imperial
War Museum archives. In 1939, over 2,900 Chinese Nationalist
troops were reported missing from their camp, just south of
Nanking. Again, men, equipment, guns, were missing through
camp fires and mess tents were undisturbed. During the
campaign, there have been instances where whole platoons and
larger units seemed to have disappeared without any sign of
combat or a struggle. Men, equipment, weapons—vanished without
a trace. In all instances the disappearances occurred in
tropical climate and in the heat of battle or near combat
zones.

3. Missing aircraft, pilots and crews, are of special concern
to the military when no explanations fit the usual reasons
outside of combat. One such incident is the disappearance of a
flight of five U.S. Navy TBM-3 Avenger torpedo bombers of a
NAS Fort Lauderdale on 5 December 1945. While no explanation from
to why navigation instruments on all five aircraft could have
failed at the same time, and efforts to rescue the 14 crewmen
were unsuccessful, it is believed that Flight 19 encountered a
phenomenon of celestial nature. The last known radio transmission
from the instructor pilot was heard by a ham operator, "Don't come
after me ... they look like they are from outer space. ... I'm
at 2,300 feet. Don't come after me." After one of the most intensive
air-sea rescue operations in U.S. Naval history, the Naval Board of
Inquiry said, we were not able to make even a good guess as to what
happened."

-13-

ANNEX C

1. Military commanders are taught a basic premise that the ideal defense as characterized by Karl von Clausewitz,—is a "shield of blows." Then an enemy attack begins the defender yields the battle ground to slow its momentum and to strike the enemy with repeated, unexpected blows. Such a defense can work, only when the enemy is detected, his strength known, his weaponry identified, and, his tactics and movements are realized.

2. In the annals of warfare mass disappearances of soldiers and their equipment are rare but are on record. In the eighteenth century during the Spanish War of Succession, 4,000 soldiers were reported to have disappeared, together with their weapons and equipment (horses included). In 1865, about 600 French colonial soldiers disappeared near Saigon, French Indo-China, without a trace of them nor their equipment. On August 21 1915, members of the New Zealand Army Corps' First Fourth Norfolk Regiment signed sworn statements that they saw the One-fourth Norfolk Regiment disappear in a unusually thick brown cloud which seemed to move and rose upward and vanished. There were no traces of the regiment nor their equipment. He explanation can be found in the historical records of the Imperial War Museum archives. In 1939, over 2,900 Chinese Nationalists troops were reported missing from their camp, just south of Nanking. Again, men, equipment, guns, were missing though camp fires and mess tents were undisturbed. During the Pacific campaign, there have been instances where whole platoons and larger units seemed to have been [...]

...of Mantell's plane was repeatedly hit by shotgun blasts. Some of the metal had pitted surfaces and unusual scoring. All rubber material had disintegrated in a soft powdery substance. There was no indication of gunfire damage or foul burn. The crash site and debris exhibited an unusually high amount of radiations/ undetermined nature. The site was cleared of debris and covered. Mantell's plane was subsequently sent to Wright-Patterson AFB, Ohio for examination. A autopsy was conducted on the body and interned in storage for future study. It is believed destroyed by the Air Force investigators that Mantell's plane had been destroyed by a ionization phenom man, possibly from the propulsion wash of the object's exhaust.

5. From 1949 to late 1950, there have been several crashes of B-36 bombers en routine arctic patrol that bear all the earmarks of the Mantell incident. None of the crews were found. The atomic bombs were not recovered, thus creating a serious problem for the Air Force when nuclear weapons are lost over friendly countries.

6. The death of two Air Force counterintelligence officers in the crash of their B-25 aircraft enroute to Hamilton AFB, California, after interviewing two auxiliary CG men who reported six UFOs over Maury Island, Washington, in June 1947. CGIC agent Crisman had spoken to Kenneth Arnold, who on 26 June 1947, had reported a flight of UFOs over Mt. Rainier, Washington, and filed his report after he had spoken to Captain Davidson and Lieutenant Brown. The material given to Davidson and Brown was believed to come from Maury Island and may be celestial fragments containing metal from a nuclear reactor from a UFO. Fragments were turned over to CIA agent Shaw and Crisman was ordered to the Alaskan ADC for assignment in Project IVY.

-11-

ANNEX C (Cont'd)

b. On 7 January 1948, a AAC P-51 pilot was lost near Godman AFB, Kentucky. After being directed to lead his flight of four P-51s by the tower, Captain Thomas Mantell pursued a large metallic object alone after two pilots returned to Godman AFB, and finally his wingman was ordered to return to the field. It is believed that Mantell was following a large, structured object not in the flight path of a classified Navy SKYHOOK balloon. Mantell radioed Godman tower that he was at 22,000 feet and still climbing. At one point Mantell said that the object had paced his aircraft for several minutes, then would speed up. His last transmission to the tower was, "It appears to be a metallic object ... and it is of tremendous size ... It appears to be a metallic object or possibly the reflection of sun from a metallic object." When Godman personnel arrived at the crash scene, Mantell's P-51 was found in many pieces, not large sections as one would find from a free stick descent. The wreckage contained unusual damage as if Mantell's plane was repeatedly hit by shotgun blasts. Some of the metal had pitted surfaces and unusual searing. All rubber material had disintegrated in a soft powdery substance. There was no indication of gunfire damage or foul burn. The crash site and debris exhibited an unusually high amount of radiation? undetermined nature. The site was cleared of debris and covered. Mantell's plane was subsequently sent to Wright-Patterson AFB, Ohio for examination. A autopsy was conducted on the body and interred in storage for future study. It is believed by the Air Force investigators that Mantell's plane had been destroyed by a ionization phenomena, possibly from the propulsion

...a collision course, the UFO flipped over sideways, crossing the flight path of Puckett's C-47. Three other crew members observed the UFO and described it as being over twice the length of a B-29 and cylindrical in shape with luminated windows. Observers on the C-47 reported a stream of fire trailing the object. The crew and Puckett watched the UFO for over three minutes. SAC radar stations had tracked a large target approaching the C-47 and then performed a right-angle course change while flying at speeds of excess of 600 mph.

9. On 1 October 1948, a AMG F-51 pilot engaged a blinking luminous UFO in a dogfight-style encounter over Fargo, North Dakota.

10. On 24 April 1949, engineers and technicians from the White Sands Proving Ground observed a elliptically-shaped object moving in a eastward course at very high altitude. The object was discovered while tracking a Skyhook balloon through a theodolite. The object appeared whitish in color and pale yellow at the tail end. The object was estimated to be two-and-a-half times as long as it was wide. It was difficult to see any structure of the object as it was moving at a very high speed. The object was observed through a theodolite for approximately one minute before disappearing in a steep climb. The object was estimated to be traveling at an altitude of over 60 miles.

-35-

208

ANNEX C (Cont'd)

7. Aerial interference with military aircraft has demonstrated the ability to observe our air operations in war and peacetime conditions. During the war there were over 900 near-miss incidents were reported by allied pilots and crews in all theater of operations. One of the most dramatic near-miss encounters occurred on 14 October 1943, 8th AF Mission 115 over Schweinfurt, Germany. B-17 crew reported many formations of silverly discs flying down into the B-17 formations. Several times during the bombing mission, large objects were seen following the discs descent into the formations. Unlike previous reports, no engine failures or airframe damage was reported. After the surrender of Nazi Germany, GAF fighter pilots were interrogated by AF intelligence concerning Mission 115. GAF did not have any aircraft above our bombers at that time.

8. On 1 August 1946, a C-47 piloted by Captain Jack E. Puckett, Assistant Chief of Flying Safety for TAC, experienced a near-miss incident of a cylindrical-shaped aircraft about 100 meters in length. The incident occurred at an altitude of 4,000 feet, northeast of Tampa, Florida, just 1,000 yards on a collision course, the UFO flipped over sideways, crossing the flight path of Puckett's C-47. Three other crew members observed the UFO and described it as being over twice the length of a B-29 and cylindrical in shape with luminated windows. Observers on the C-47 reported a stream of fire trailing the object. The crew and Puckett watched the UFO for over three minutes. TAC radar stations had tracked a large target approaching the C-47 and then performed a right-angle course change while flying at speeds of excess of 600 mph.

9. On 1 October 1948, a ANG F-51 pilot engaged a blinking luminous
UFO in a dogfight.

APPENDIX B

On the following pages is the letter entitled "Relationships with Inhabitants of Celestial Bodies" by Dr. Robert J. Oppenheimer and Albert Einstein.

they should have a psychology similar to that of men.

At any rate, International law should make place for a new law on a different basis, and it might be called "Law Among Planetary Peoples," following the guidelines found in the Pentateuch. Obviously, the idea of revolutionizing International law to the point where it would be capable of coping with new situations would compel us to make a change in its structure, a change so basic that it would no longer be International law, that is to say, as it is conceived today, but something altogether different, so that it could no longer bear the same name.

If these intelligent beings were in possession of a more or less culture, and a more or less perfect political organization, they would have an absolute right to be recognized as independent and sovereign peoples; we would have to come to an agreement with them to establish the legal regulations upon which future relationships should be based, and it would be necessary to accept many of their principles.

Finally, if they should reject all peaceful cooperation and become an imminent threat to the earth, we would have the right to legitimate defense, but only insofar as would be necessary to annul this danger.

*****

Another possibility may exist, that a species of homo sapiens might have established themselves as an independent nation on another celestrial body in our solar system and

-1-

DRAFT June 1947

Relationships with Inhabitants of Celestial Bodies

Relationships with extraterrestrial men presents no basically new problem from the standpoint of international law; but the possibility of confronting intelligent beings that do not belong to the human race would bring up problems whose solution it is difficult to conceive.

In principle, there is no difficulty in accepting the possibility of coming to an understanding with them, and of establishing all kinds of relationships. The difficulty lies in trying to establish the principles on which these relationships should be based.

In the first place, it would be necessary to establish communication with them through some language or other, and afterwards, as a first condition for all intelligence, that they should have a psychology similar to that of men.

At any rate, international law should make place for a new law on a different basis, and it might be called "Law Among Planetary Peoples," following the guidelines found in the Pentateuch. Obviously, the idea of revolutionizing international law to the point where it would be capable of coping with new situations would compel us to make a change in its structure, a change so basic that it would no longer be international law, that is to say, as it is conceived could be used for breathing purposes; the hydrogen might be used as a fuel.

In any case, if no existence is possible on celestial bodies except for enterprises for the exploration of their natural riches, with a continuous interchange of the men who work on them, unable to establish themselves there indefinitely and be able to live isolated life, independence will never take place.

*****

Now we come to the problem of determining what to do if the inhabitants of celestial bodies, or extraterrestrial biological entities (EBE) desire to settle here.

1. If they are politically organized and possess a certain culture similar to our own, they may be recognized as a independent people. They could consider what degree of development would be required on earth for colonizing.

2. If they consider our culture to devoid of political unity, they would have the right to colonize. Of course, this colonization cannot be conducted on classic lines.

A superior form of colonizing will have to be conceived, that could be a kind of tutelage, possibly through the tacit approval of the United Nations. But would the United Nations legally have the right of allowing such tutelage over us in such a fashion?

-2-

evolved culturely independently from ours. Obviously this
possiblity depends on many circumstances, whose conditions
cannot yet be foreseen. However, we can make a study of the
basis on which such a thing might have occurred.

In the first place, living conditions on these bodies
lets say the moon, or the planet Mars, would have to be such
as to permit a stable, and to a certain extent, independent
life, from an economic standpoint. Much has been speculated
about the possiblities for life existing outside of our
atmosphere and beyond, always hypothetically and there are
those who go so far as to give formulas for the creation of
an artificial atmosphere on the moon, which undoubtedly have
a certain scientific foundation, and which may one day come
to light. Lets assume that magnesium silicates on the moon
may exist and contain up to 13 per cent water. Using energy
and machines brought to the moon, perhaps from a space station,
the rocks could be broken up, pulverized, and then backed to
drive off the water of crystallization. This could be collected
and then decomposed into hydrogen and oxygen, using an electric
current or the short wave radiation of the sun. The oxygen
could be used for breathing purposes; the hydrogen might be
used as a fuel.

In any case, if no existence is possible on celestrial
bodies except for enterprises for the exploration of their
natural riches, with a continuous interchange of the men who
work on them, unable to establish themselves there indefinitely
and be able to live isolated life, independence will never

international law will be with regard to the occupation by celestial peoples of certain locations on our planet; but the only thing that can be foreseen is that there will be a profound change in traditional concepts.

We cannot exclude the possibility that a race of extraterrestrial people more advanced technologically and economically may take upon itself the right to occupy another celestial body. How, then, would this occupation come about?

1. The idea of exploitation by one celestial state would be rejected, they may think it would be advisable to grant it to all others capable of reaching another celestial body. But this would be to maintain a situation of privilege for these states.

2. The division of a celestial body into zones and the distribution of them among other celestial states. This would present the problem of distribution. Moreover, other celestial states would be deprived of the possibility of owning an area, or if they were granted one it would involve complicated operations.

3. Indivisible co-sovereignty, giving each celestial state the right to make whatever use is most convenient to its interests, independently of the others. This would create a situation of anarchy, as the strongest one would win out in the end.

4. A moral entity? The most feasible solution it

(a) Although the United Nations is an international organization, there is no doubt that it would have no right of tutelage, since its domain does not extend beyond relationships between its members. It would have the right to intervene only if the relationships of a member nation with a celestial body affected another member nation with an extraterrestrial people is beyond the domain of the United Nations. But if these relationships entailed a conflict with another member nation, the United Nations would have the right to intervene.

(b) If the United Nations were a supra-national organization, it would have competency to deal with all problems related to extraterrestrial peoples. Of course, even though it is merely an international organization, it could have this competence if its member states would be willing to recognize it.

*****

It is difficult to predict what the attitude of international law will be with regard to the occupation by celestial peoples of certain locations on our planet; but the only thing that can be foreseen is that there will be a profound change in traditional concepts.

We cannot exclude the possibility that a race of extraterrestrial people more advanced technologically and economically may take upon itself the right to occupy another celestial body. How, then, would this occupation come about?

until the last century, occupation was the normal
means of acquiring sovereignty over territories, when
explorations made possible the discovery of new regions,
either uninhabited or in an elementary state of civilization.

The imperialist expansion of the states came to an
end with the end of regions capable of being occupied, which
have now been drained from the earth and exist only in
interplanetary space, where the celestial states present
new problems.

*****

Res nullius is something that belongs to nobody such
as the moon. In international law a celestial body is not
subject to the sovereignty of any state is considered _res
nullius_. If it could be established that a celestial body
within our solar system such as our moon was, or is occupied
by another celestial race, there could be no claim of _res
nullius_ by any state on earth (if that state should decide
in the future to send explorers to lay claim to it). It would
exist as _res communis_, that is that all celestial states
have the same rights over it.

*****

And now to the final question of whether the presence
of celestial astroplanes in our atmosphere is a direct
result of our testing atomic weapons?

The presence of unidentified space craft flying in
our atmosphere (and possibly maintaining orbits about our
planet) is now, however, accepted by our military. ..

—4—

usdf=facto

seem would be this one, submit an agreement providing for the
peaceful absorption of a celestial race(s) in such a manner
that our culture would remain intact with guarantees that
their presence not be revealed.

Actually, we do not believe it necessary to go that
far. It would merely be a matter of internationalizing
celestial peoples, and creating an international treaty
instrument preventing exploitation of all nations belonging
to the United Nations.

#####

Occupation by states here on earth, which has lost
all interest for international law, since there were no more
res nullius territories, is beginning to regain all its
importance in cosmic international law.

Occupation consists in the appropriation by a state
of res nullius.

Until the last century, occupation was the normal
means of acquiring sovereignty over territories, when
explorations made possible the discovery of new regions,
either uninhabited or in an elementary state of civilization.

The imperialist expansion of the states came to an
end with the end of regions capable of being occupied, which
have now been drained from the earth and exist only in
interplanetary space, where the celestial states present
new problems.

219

...the ...oyment of artificial satellites for intelligence gathering and target selection is not far off. The military importance of space vehicles, satellites as well as rockets is indisputable, since they project war from the horizontal plane to the vertical plane in its fullest sense. Attack no longer comes from an exclusive direction, nor from a determined country, but from the sky, with the practical impossibility of determining who the aggressor is, how to intercept the attack, or how to effect immediate reprisals. These problems are compounded further by identification. How does the air defense radar operator identify, or more precisely, classify his target?

At present, we can breath a little easier knowing that slow moving bombers are the mode of delivery of atomic bombs that can be detected by long-range early warning radar. But what do we do in lets say ten years from now? When artificial satellites and missiles find their place in space, we must consider the potential threat that unidentified space craft pose. One must consider the fact that mis-identification of these space craft for a intercontenental missile in a re-entry phase of flight could lead to accidental nuclear war with horrible consequences.

Lastly, we should consider the possibility that our atmospheric tests of late could have influenced the arrival of celestrial scrutiny. They could have been curious or even alarmed by such activity (and rightly so, for the Russians would make every effort to observe and record such tests).

In conclusion, it is our professional opinion based on submitted data that this situation is extremely perilous, and

-5-

On every question of whether the United States will continue testing of fission bombs and develop fusion devices (hydrogen bombs), or reach an agreement to disarm and the exclusion of weapons that are too destructive, with the exception of chemical warfare, on which, by some miracle we cannot explain, an agreement has been reached, the lamentations of philosophers, the efforts of politicians, and the conferences of diplomats have been doomed to failure and have accomplished nothing.

The use of the atomic bomb combined with space vehicles poses a threat on a scale which makes it absolutely necessary to come to an agreement in this area. With the appearance of unidentified space vehicles (opinions are sharply divided as to their origin) over the skies of Europe and the United States has sustained an ineradical fear, an anxiety about security, that is driving the great powers to make an effort to find a solution to the threat.

Military strategists foresee the use of space craft with nuclear warheads as the ultimate weapon of war. Even the deployment of artificial satellites for intelligence gathering and target selection is not far off. The military importance of space vehicles, satellites as well as rockets is indisputable, since they project war from the horizontal plane to the vertical plane in its fullest sense. Attack no longer comes from an exclusive direction, nor from a determined country, but from the sky, with the practical impossibility of determining who the aggressor is, how to intercept the attack, or how to effect immediate reprisals. These problems are compounded further by identification.

Princeton, New Jersey

-6-

Myself and Mrs. ... have read t...s and I must admit there
is some doubt. But I have think the ... results will consider
it for the obvious reasons. I understand Oppenheimer
approached Marshall who ... they attended recently at

As I understand it Marshall rebuffed the idea
of Oppenheimer very discussing this with the President. I asked
to Gordon, and he agreed.

TOP SECRET

measures must be taken to rectify a very serious problem are
very apparent.

Respectfully,

/s/

Dr. J. Robert Oppenheimer
Director of Advanced Studies
Princeton, New Jersey

/s/

Professor Albert Einstein
Princeton, New Jersey

APPENDIX C

During the last few years, hundreds of documents relating to UFO's have been released. They have dribbled out for years, but recently thousands have been obtained. They relate a tale and deception that began in July 1947 and has lasted until today. The few documents that follow are a representative sample of the material that investigators have uncovered with FOIA (the Freedom of Information Act) requests, library searches, and queries to official organizations. There are literally thousands of such documents now, but these demonstrate better than most that UFO's are real and the Government knows it.

To make these easier to read, the content of each document has been written out in easy to read English on the opposite page from the original copy.

0020120

MAJIC EYES ONLY (crossed out)

Total pages -- 19　　　　　　　Copy No. MJ-7
No. 0001 - 19 September 1947

By Auth.
Date　　　　9 July 1947
Initials
　　　　　　　　September 24, 1947

NOTE: No one without express permission from the President, may disseminate the information contained in this Report or communicate it to any unauthorized person not possessing MAJIC SECURITY CLEARANCE.

Those authorized to disseminate such information must employ the most secure means, must take every precaution to avoid compromising sources, and must limit dissemination to the minimum number of secure and responsible persons who have a "need to know" in order to discharge their responsibility.

No action is to be taken on information herein reported, regardless of temporary advantage, if such action might have the effect of revealing the existence of such information to foreign intelligence agencies who might exploit for reasons of endangering national security interests.

Foreign powers not amicable to strategic national security interests will attempt to exploit such information in the possession of the United States Government. They do not know and must not be permitted to learn, either the degree of our accomplishment or the particular source from which any technological advances (blacked out) in this report.

0020120

MAJIC EYES ONLY

Total pages-- 19

Copy No. MJ-7

No. 0001 - 19 September 1947

By Auth.
Date   7 JULY 1947
Initials

Approved

Harry Truman

September 24, 1947

Iam Keeping for further study.

A.C. Wedemeyer

NOTE: No one, without express permission from the President, may disseminate the information contained in this Report or communicate it to any unauthorized person not possessing MAJI SECURITY CLEARANCE.

These authorized to disseminate such information must employ only the most secure means, must take every precaution to avoid compromising sources, and must limit dissemination to the minimum number of secure and responsible persons who have a "need to know" in order to discharge their responsibility

No action is to be taken on information herein reported, regardless of temporary advantage, if such action might have the effect of revealing the existence of such information to foreign intelligence agencies who might exploit for reasons of endangering national security interests.

Foreign powers not amicable to to strategic national security interests will attempt to exploit such information in the possession of the United States Government. They do not know and must not be permitted to learn, either the degree of our accomplishment or the particular source from which any technological advances ████████████████████████████████ in this report.

MAJIC EYES ONLY

227

TOP SECRET/MAJIC EYES ONLY
<u>EYES ONLY</u>   Copy 1 of 1

Ref: 'MAJIC'   Cryptographic security does not apply -
      EO 092447 Handle as TOP SECURITY correspon-
      MJ-12 Rpt dence per Par 44-G and 53-A AR 380-5
      19 SEP '47
                         September 25, 1947

<u>MEMORANDUM FOR THE PRESIDENT</u>

The following letter from Secretary Marshall to the President was dictated to me this morning over the secret telephone:

"Dear Mr. President:

"I understand General Twining is presenting his report to you at sometime today. It seems to me mandatory that we treat Twining's report top secret and that no indication to its contents be divulged to the public. This will allow us time to review our policy in the light of the report.

"If you agree, I suggest Twining be informed by you accordingly.

"If questioned, you might state a cover summary of the report be issued until careful consideration has been given it by the various chiefs of staff and department heads of the Government concerned.

                         Faithfully yours,
                         G.C. MARSHALL

                         C.H. Homalzine
                         Executive Secretary

TOP SECRET / MAJIC
EYES ONLY

EYES ONLY

Copy 1 of 1

Ref: "MAJIC"
EO 092447
MJ-12 Rpt
19 SEP 'M7

Cryptographic security does not apply —
Handle as TOP SECRET correspondence per
Par 44-G and 53-A AR 380-5

September 25, 1947

MEMORANDUM FOR THE PRESIDENT

The following letter from Secretary Marshall to the President was dictated to me this morning over the secret telephone:

"Dear Mr. President:

"I understand General Twining is presenting his report to you at sometime today. It seems to me mandatory that we treat Twining's report top secret and that no indication to its contents be divulged to the public. This will allow us time to review our policy in the light of the report.

"If you agree, I suggest Twining be informed by you accordingly.

"If questioned, you might state a cover summary of the report be issued until careful consideration has been given it by the various chiefs of staff and department heads of the Government concerned.

Faithfully yours,
G.G. MARSHALL"

C.H. Humelsine
Executive Secretary

RECEIVED

OCT 0 7 1992

EYES ONLY

TOP SECRET / MAJIC
EYES ONLY

229

The White House

Washington

TOP SECRET   June 28, 1961

NATIONAL SECURITY MEMORANDUM

TO: The Director, Central Intelligence Agency

SUBJECT: Review of MJ-12 Intelligence Operations as they relate to Cold War Psychological Warfare Plans

I would like a brief summary from you at your earliest convenience.

TOP SECRET

THE WHITE HOUSE

WASHINGTON

DISPATCHED
N. S. C.

TOP SECRET   Jun 29 3 ·· PM '61   June 28, 1961

NATIONAL SECURITY MEMORANDUM

TO: The Director, Central Intelligence Agency

SUBJECT: Review of MJ-12 Intelligence Operations as they relate to
         Cold War Psychological Warfare Plans

     I would like a brief summary from you at your earliest convenience.

TOP SECRET

[signature]

July 14, 1954

<u>TOP SECRET RESTRICTED</u>
<u>SECURITY INFORMATION</u>

MEMORANDUM FOR GENERAL TWINING

SUBJECT: (illegible)/MJ-12 Special Studies Project

The President has decided that the MJ-12 SSP brief-ing should take place <u>during</u> the already scheduled White House meeting of July 16, rather than following it as previously intended. More precise arrangements will be explained to you upon arrival. Please alter your plans accordingly.

Your concurrence in the above change of arrange-ments is assumed.

ROBERT CUTLER
Special Assistant
to the President

July 14, 1954

MEMORANDUM FOR GENERAL TWINING

SUBJECT: NSC/MJ-12 Special Studies Project

The President has decided that the MJ-12 SSP briefing should take place during the already scheduled White House meeting of July 16, rather than following it as previously intended. More precise arrangements will be explained to you upon arrival. Please alter your plans accordingly.

Your concurrence in the above change of arrangements is assumed.

ROBERT CUTLER
Special Assistant
to the President

APPENDIX D

On page 236 and 237 is one of the most convincing Government documents yet to surface as regards official knowledge of alien visitors. The reference to high powered radar interfering with the controlling mechanisms has long been forwarded as a theory by Preston Nichols. He ought to know as he an expert in such systems.

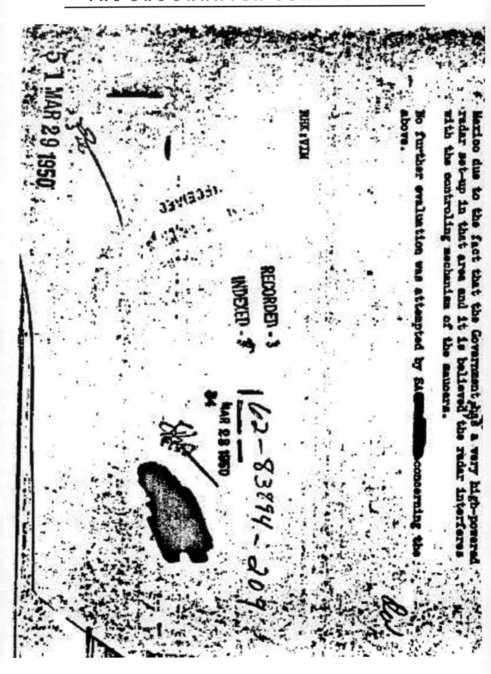

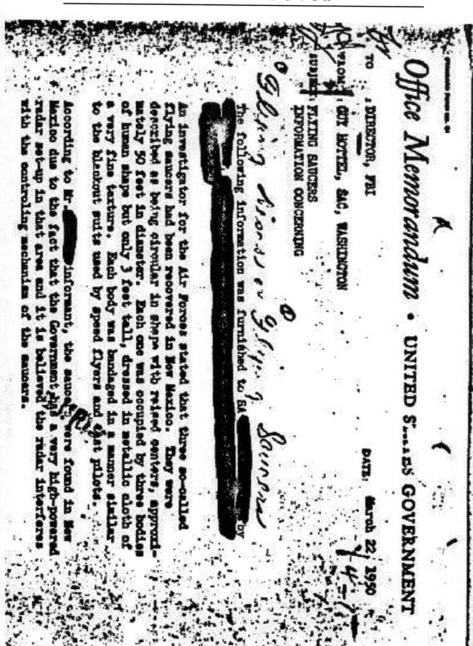

Office Memorandum • UNITED STATES GOVERNMENT

TO : DIRECTOR, FBI

FROM : GUY HOTTEL, SAC, WASHINGTON

SUBJECT: FLYING SAUCERS
INFORMATION CONCERNING

DATE: March 22, 1950

The following information was furnished to SA [redacted] by [redacted].

An investigator for the Air Forces stated that three so-called flying saucers had been recovered in New Mexico. They were described as being circular in shape with raised centers, approximately 50 feet in diameter. Each one was occupied by three bodies of human shape but only 3 feet tall, dressed in metallic cloth of a very fine texture. Each body was bandaged in a manner similar to the blackout suits used by speed flyers and test pilots.

According to Mr. [redacted] informant, the saucers were found in New Mexico due to the fact that the Government has a very high-powered radar set-up in that area and it is believed the radar interferes with the controlling mechanism of the saucers.

INDEX

The Search for Ong's Hat

by Peter Moon

Since Peter Moon's involvement in the Montauk investigation, he has encountered incredible synchronicities with regard to space-time projects and clans of mystery. None of these have been more riveting than his encounter with the mysterious legend of Ong's Hat, a real but enigmatic location in south central New Jersey that was once used by Princeton physicists as a post office return address for dissident physics papers submitted under assumed names. In addition to serving as the adopted postal home for certain scientists from the Institute for Advanced Studies (where von Neumann and Einstein and others are said to have hatched the Philadelphia Experiment), Ong's Hat was also the home of a mysterious ashram whose roots were connected to an even more mysterious Moorish Science Temple. This ashram was an environment with both scientific and natural features that included a hodgepodge of Tantra, Sufism, Ismaili esotericism, alchemy, psychopharmacology, biofeedback and brain machine meditation techniques. All of this focused on the theory that consciousness itself could be presented as a set of "strange attractors" (could also be called "patterns of chaos" or "coherent units of attractions") around which specific neuronal activity would organize itself. Keeping in mind that these attractors were not necessarily relegated to this dimension only, the players sought patterns or "mind maps" through the actual geometry of the attractors themselves. By grasping these shapes both intuitively and non-intuitively, one could learn to "ride with chaos" much like a lucid dreamer learns to direct the process of REM sleep. The experiments and theories suggested a mind boggling array of benefits such as links between cybernetic processes and awareness itself, including exploration of the brains unused capacities, awareness of the morphogenetic field and thus conscious control of autonomic functions such as repair of tissue and aging. Eventually, the entire operation became a gate to other dimensions and worlds whereupon Ong's Hat became known as the depot for a time-travel cult that is said to move in and out of this dimension. Up to now, the truth about the cult has been vague and indecisive, but the legends, technology and quantum theory surrounding the cult have been more than tangible.

In his most ambitious work to date, Peter Moon summates and synthesizes his own experiences with synchronicity and accelerates this process to an unparalleled level as he interfaces with the cult's representatives which results in an explosion of new information and an excursion into previously unchartered territory.

Currently, this is a work in progress which is not sheduled to be completed as a manuscript until early 2002. Publication is planned sometime in that year.

This advertisement is being written one day after the World Trade Center bombing in New York, the full impact of which has yet to be realized. Changes are occurring on a mass scale in our environment. As the truth unfolds, tyranny is exposed, the tentacles of which are interwoven deeply into our society and its institutions through the most subtle and secretive methods imaginable. One of these institutions is the book industry which distributes information to the masses. In the interest of overturning this tyranny, ample consideration has been given to boycotting Peter Moon's new work from established means in order to avoid impedence of the message contained therein. Therefore, this may be a rare book that will only be sold through the publisher and selected mail order catalogs and websites. A final de-termination has yet to be made. Another possibility be-ing considered is to put a much higher price on the books sold to the regular book trade whereas the catalog price would be much more reasonable. All of this is being considered to combat the inflationary pressures in the book industry and the attrition factor that is currently work-ing to eliminate small presses such as Sky Books.

Therefore, if you are interested in this new publica-tion, and you are not already on the Sky Books mailing list or a subscriber to *The Montauk Pulse*, send your name and address to the following address in order to receive a flyer when this new book becomes available.

Sky Books
PO Box 769
Westbury, NY 11590

It should also be noted that "The Search for Ong's Hat" is a working title and that a final decision has not been rendered on that as well. Updates on the status of this book will be given periodically in the newsletter *The Montauk Pulse*.

THE ULTIMATE PROOF

*P*yramids of Montauk: Explorations In Consciousness awakens the consciousness of humanity to its ancient history and origins through the discovery of pyramids at Montauk and their placement on sacred Native American ground leading to an unprecedented investigation of the mystery schools of Earth and their connection to Egypt, Atlantis, Mars and the star Sirius. An astonishing sequel to the *Montauk Project* and *Montauk Revisited*, this chapter of the legend propels us far beyond the adventures of the first two books and stirs the quest for future reality and the end of time as we know it.

256 pages, illustrations, photos and diagrams.............$19.95

THE BLACK SUN

*I*n this spectacular addition to the Montauk series, *The Black Sun* continues the intriguing revelations readers have come to expect revealing Montauk's Nazi connection and a vast array of new information. From the German flying saucer program to the SS Tibet mission, we are led on a path that gives us the most insightful look ever into the Third Reich and their ultimate quest: the Ark of the Covenant and the Holy Grail. Going beyond *The Spear of Destiny* and other attempts to unlock the mysterious occultism of the Nazis, Peter Moon peers into the lab of the ancient alchemists in order to explain the secret meaning behind the Egyptian and Tibetan "Books of the Dead."

295 pages, illustrations, photos......................................$19.95

Journey to the stars
with Preston Nichols & Peter Moon's
ENCOUNTER IN THE PLEIADES

The incredible story of a man who found himself taken to the Pleiades for a scientific education far beyond the horizons of anything taught in universities. For the first time, Preston Nichols reveals his personal history with an avalanche of amazing information including a new look at Einstein and the history of physics which gives unprecedented insight into the technology of flying saucers and their accompanying phenomena. Never before has the complex subject of UFO's been explained in such a simple language that will be appreciated by the scientist and understood by the layman. Peter Moon adds further intrigue to the mix by revealing the role of the Pleiades in ancient mythology and sheds new light on the current predicament of Mankind and offers a path of hope for the future. The truth is revealed. The keys to the Pleiades are in hand and the gateway to the stars is open. 252 pages...$19.95

The Alien Connection

Montauk: The Alien Connection reveals the most amazing story yet to surface in the area of alien abduction. This is an autobiographical and factual account from Stewart Swerdlow, a gifted mentalist who was born clairvoyant but haunted by strange time-space scenarios. After suffering alien abductions and government manipulations, Stewart found Preston Nichols and discovered his own role in time travel experiments known as the Montauk Project. After refusing to break his association with Nichols, Stewart was incarcerated by the authorities, but the truth began to reveal itself. Struggling for his life, Stewart used his mental abilities to overcome the negative influences surrounding him and ultimately discovered the highest common denominator in the alien equation — an interdimensional language which communicates to all conscious beings. This an intriguing new twist to the Montauk saga which elevates the entire subject to a higher octave. 252 pages..$19.95

The Healer's Handbook

The miraculous and strange become common place as you journey out of this dimension with Stewart Swerdlow and discover the Language of Hyperspace, a simple system of geometric and archetypal glyphs enabling us to comprehend universal mysteries ranging from crop circles to the full panorama of occult science. *The Healer's Handbook: A Journey Into Hyperspace* penetrates the secrets of creation through the mysterious principles of DNA, the biological interface between spirit and matter which determines our actual physical characteristics and maladies. *The Healer's Handbook: A Journey Into Hyperspace* shows a vast panorama of healing techniques and supplementary information including: color healing, dream analysis, numeric values and symbols, auric fields, astral and hyperspace travel, prayer, meditation techniques, and radionics as well as exercises designed to unlock DNA sequences programmed within you since the beginning. 152 pages, 8 1/2" by 11", with diagrams and color chart.......$22.00

The Music of Time

The Music of Time blends music with time travel as Preston Nichols reveals his hidden role in the music industry where he engineered hundreds of hit records during the Golden Era of Rock 'n Roll. Beginning with his work for Time Records, Preston chronicles his innovations in sound engineering and tells how he constructed the premier music studio in the world. Having created a Mecca for talented musicians, Preston found himself surrounded by the likes of the Beatles, Beach Boys, Rolling Stones, and many popular acts. Music, mind control, and time travel make for a strange and fascinating mix with Preston's real life adventures leading to him becoming a marked man who barely escapes with his life. **The Music of Time** unravels more layers of mystery in mankind's epic quest to understand the paradox of time and the imprisonment of consciousness. 252 pages..........................$19.95

THE PHILADELPHIA EXPERIMENT MURDER: PARALLEL UNIVERSES AND THE PHYSICS OF INSANITY

By Alexandra Bruce
Edited by Peter Moon

The Philadelphia Experiment Murder: Parallel Universes and the Physics of Insanity is the latest edition in the intriguing series by Sky Books which exposes the truth about the conspiracy to manipulate time itself. This new book, edited and contributed to by Peter Moon and authored by Alexandra Bruce, begins with the tragic murder of conspiracy lecturer Phil Schneider. An investigation of this murder exposes a massive cover-up by authorities and reveals astonishing information, the trail of which leads back to the Philadelphia Experiment of 1943. Before his assassination, Schneider lectured across the country and released documents connecting his father to the *U.S.S. Eldridge.* Additionally, his father claimed to be a Nazi U-boat captain who, after being captured by the Allies, was recruited as a medical officer and served as a Senior Medical Officer to the crew of the *Eldridge.* More haunting was the discovery of gold bars in his father's possessions with Nazi insignia. *The Philadelphia Experiment Murder: Parallel Universes and the Physics of Insanity* investigates these circumstances and uncovers a host of new characters including Preston Nichols' boss from the Montauk Project. Startling truths are revealed which lead to an examination of parallel universes and the nature of insanity itself. *The Philadelphia Experiment Murder* not only exposes the murder of an innocent man, but the effort to murder the truth itself. *256 pages* $19.95

The Montauk Pulse™
A CHRONICLE OF TIME

A newsletter by the name of *The Montauk Pulse* went into print in the winter of 1993 to chronicle the events and discoveries regarding the ongoing investigation of the Montauk Project by Preston Nichols and Peter Moon. It has remained in print and been issued quarterly ever since. With a minimum of six pages and a distinct identity of its own, *The Pulse* will often comment on details and history that do not necessarily find their way into books.

Through 2002, The *Montauk Pulse* has included exciting new breakthroughs on the Montauk story as well as similarly related phenomena like the Philadelphia Experiment, Brookhaven Connection or other space-time projects. Coverage on the Brookhaven investigation will continue.

Subscribing to *The Pulse* directly contributes to the efforts of the authors in writing more books and chronicling the effort to understand time and all of its components. Past support has been crucial to our continued existence. We appreciate your support in helping to unravel various mysteries of Earth-based and non-Earth-based consciousness. It makes a difference.

SHIPPING INFORMATION

United States Shipping

Under $30.00 ....add $3.50
$30.01 — 60.00 ...add $4.50
$60.00 — $100.00 add $6.50
$100.01 and over ..add $8.50

Allow 30 days for delivery. For U.S. only: Priority Mail—add the following to the regular shipping charge: $4.00 for first item, $1.50 for each additional item.

Outside U.S. Shipping

Under $30.00.........add $9.00
$30.01 — $50.00..add $13.00
$50.01—$ 75.00 ..add $16.00
$75.01—$100.00 .add $20.00
100.01 and over...add $25.00

These rates are for SURFACE SHIP-PING ONLY. Do *not* add extra funds for air mail. Due to the vastly different costs for each country, we will not ship by air. Only Visa, Mastercard or checks drawn on a U.S. bank in U.S. funds will be accepted. (Eurochecks or Postal Money Orders cannot be accepted.)

SkyBooks   ORDER FORM

*We wait for ALL checks to clear before shipping. This includes Priority Mail orders.
If you want to speed delivery time, please send a U.S. Money Order or use
MasterCard or Visa. Those orders will be shipped right away.
Complete this order form and send with payment or credit card information to:
Sky Books, Box 769, Westbury, New York 11590-0104*

Name	
Address	
City	
State / Country	**Zip**
Daytime Phone (In case we have a question) ( )	

☐ **This is my first order**   ☐ **I have ordered before**   ☐ **This is a new address**

Method of Payment: ☐ **Visa**   ☐ **MasterCard**   ☐ **Money Order**   ☐ **Check**

_____ — _____ — _____ —

Expiration Date   **Signature**

Title	Qty	Price
The Montauk Pulse (1 year subscription)......................$12.00		
The Montauk Pulse back issues (List at bottom of page.) $3.00 each		
List:		
Subtotal		
For delivery in NY add 8.5% tax		
Shipping: see chart on the next page		
U.S. only: Priority Mail		
Total		

Thank you for your order. We appreciate your business.